The Book of the West Highland White Terrier
TS-187

West Highland White Terriers owned by the Kompares.

Title page: Best in Show **Ch. Kilkerran D'Artagnon**, bred and owned by Kathy and Wayne Kompare, Danbury, CT. By Ch. Cynosure Orion The Hunter ex Ch. Kortni of Windy Hill.

Dedication

In fond memory of Mrs. D. J.,
a wonderful friend of this breed
sadly missed by us all.

Anna

Distributed in the UNITED STATES to the Pet Trade by T.F.H. Publications, Inc., One T.F.H. Plaza, Neptune City, NJ 07753; distributed in the UNITED STATES to the Bookstore and Library Trade by National Book Network, Inc. 4720 Boston Way, Lanham MD 20706; in CANADA to the Pet Trade by H & L Pet Supplies Inc., 27 Kingston Crescent, Kitchener, Ontario N2B 2T6; Rolf C. Hagen Ltd., 3225 Sartelon Street, Montreal 382 Quebec; in CANADA to the Book Trade by Macmillan of Canada (A Division of Canada Publishing Corporation), 164 Commander Boulevard, Agincourt, Ontario M1S 3C7; in ENGLAND by T.F.H. Publications, PO Box 15, Waterlooville PO7 6BQ; in AUSTRALIA AND THE SOUTH PACIFIC by T.F.H. (Australia), Pty. Ltd., Box 149, Brookvale 2100 N.S.W., Australia; in NEW ZEALAND by Brooklands Aquarium Ltd., 5 McGiven Drive, New Plymouth, RD1 New Zealand; in the PHILIPPINES by Bio-Research, 5 Lippay Street, San Lorenzo Village, Makati, Rizal; in SOUTH AFRICA by Multipet Pty. Ltd., P.O. Box 35347, Northway, 4065, South Africa. Published by T.F.H. Publications, Inc. Manufactured in the United States of America by T.F.H. Publications, Inc.

The Book of the West Highland White Terrier

Anna Katherine Nicholas

Ch. Kilkerran The Joker is Wild completed his title at age 13 months having taken his points at prestigious events including two specialties. Owned by Kathy and Wayne Kompare; co-owned by Brian Forrow.

Contents

The star is risen, at age six months, **Crinan Christmas Sno** wins Best Puppy in Show at the WHWTC Specialty in England. Sno was bred by Great Britain's renowned artist, judge and breeder Barbara Hands. In addition to this pictured win, Sno has the distinction of having won the *Dog World* Puppy of the Year Regional Puppy Stakes at Leeds, an all-breed show with an entry of 11,000. She is the first Westie to have won this coveted competition in many years. Sno left England just in time to arrive for the Montgomery County Terrier Show in Pennsylvania on October 4, 1992. Her new owners in the United States are Wayne and Kathy Kompare of Kilkerran Kennels, Danbury, CT, at whose home she will join some of our most distinguished winners.

Sno is a daughter of Eng. Ch. Clan Crinan, and she is accompanied to her new home by her litter sister, Crinan Christmas Carol. It is interesting to note that these two are full-sisters to the multiple English-bred Best in Show winner Ch. Crinan Counterpoint owned by the Marumotos who now live in Hawaii.

About the Author

Since early childhood, Anna Katherine Nicholas has been involved with dogs. Her first pets were a Boston Terrier, an Airedale, and a German Shepherd Dog. Then, in 1925, came the first of the Pekingese, a gift from a friend who raised them. Now her home is shared with two Miniature Poodles and numerous Beagles.

Miss Nicholas is best known throughout the dog fancy as a writer and as a judge. Her first magazine article, published in *Dog News* magazine around 1930, was about Pekingese, and this was followed by a widely acclaimed breed column, "Peeking at the Pekingese," which appeared for at least two decades, originally in *Dogdom*, then, following

Merriwest Lady Guinevere winning Best of Breed under the author at Troy K.C. in 1988. Owner-handled by Marian Maeller.

the demise of that publication, in *Popular Dogs*. During the 1940s she was a Boxer columnist for *Pure-Bred Dogs/American Kennel Gazette* and for *Boxer Briefs*. More recently many of her articles, geared to interest fanciers of every breed, have appeared in *Pure-Bred Dogs / American Kennel Gazette, Show Dogs, Dog Fancy, The World of the Working Dog*, and for both the Canadian publications *The Dog Fancier* and *Dogs in Canada*. Her *Dog World* column, "Here, There and Everywhere," was the Dog Writers' Association of America winner of the Best Series in a Dog Magazine Award for 1979. Another feature article of hers, "Faster Is Not Better," published in *Canine Chronicle*, received Honorable Mention on another occasion.

In 1970 Miss Nicholas won the Dog Writers' Association Award for the Best Technical Book of the Year with her *Nicholas Guide to Dog Judging*. In 1979 the revision of this book again won this award, the first time ever that a revision had been so honored by this organization. Other important dog writer awards which Miss Nicholas has gained over the years have been the Gaines "Fido" and the *Kennel Review* "Winkies," these both on two occasions and each in the Dog Writer of the Year category.

One of the famed winning Westies from Shelburne Kennels, Mr. and Mrs. George Seemann, Jr., South Norwalk, CT. This dog is **Ch. Kilbrannon Curtain Up,** who came from England to the United States. Before completing the title he won two Terrier Groups and was Best of Winners at the 1980 Montgomery All-Terrier Show. He has multiple Group placements and is a successful sire.

It was during the 1930s that Miss Nicholas's first book, *The Pekingese*, appeared in print, published by the Judy Publishing Company. This book, and its second edition, sold out quickly and is now a collector's item, as is *The Skye Terrier Book* which was published during the 1960s by the Skye Terrier Club of America.

During recent years, Miss Nicholas has been writing books consistently for T.F.H. These include *Successful Dog Show Exhibiting, The Book of the Rottweiler, The Book of the Poodle, The Book of the Labrador Retriever, The Book of the English Springer Spaniel, The Book of the Golden Retriever, The Book of the German Shepherd Dog, The Book of the Shetland Sheepdog, The Book of the Miniature Schnauzer, The World of Doberman Pinschers,* and *The World of Rottweilers.* Plus, in another T.F.H. series, *The Maltese, The Keeshond, The Chow Chow, The Poodle, The Boxer, The Beagle, The Basset Hound, The Dachshund* (the latter three co-authored with Marcia A. Foy), *The German Pointer, The Collie, The Weimaraner, The Great Dane, The Dalmatian,* and numerous other titles. In the KW series she has done *Rottweilers, Weimaraners,* and *Norwegian Elkhounds.*

Portrait of a favorite Westie by Dorothy Hardcastle. The important winner, **Ch. Braidholme White Tornado of Binate**, bred by J. Morrow, owned by Mr. and Mrs. George Seemann, Jr.

And she has written American chapters for two popular English books purchased and published in the United States by T.F.H., *The Staffordshire Bull Terrier* and *The Jack Russell Terrier*.

Miss Nicholas's association with T.F.H. began in the early 1970s when she co-authored five books with Joan Brearley: *The Wonderful World of Beagles and Beagling* (also honored by the Dog Writers Association), *This is the Bichon Frise*, *The Book of the Pekingese*, *The Book of the Boxer*, and *This is the Skye Terrier*.

Best in Show **Ch. Kilkerran D'Artagnon,** by Ch. Cynosure Orion the Hunter ex Ch. Kortni of Windy Hill, is a homebred owned by Kathy and Wayne Kompare.

Miss Nicholas most recently has authored new books on some of the world's most recognizable dogs, included among these are *The Professional's Book of Rottweilers*, *The World of the Chinese Shar-Pei* and *The Staffordshire Terriers*.

Since 1934 Miss Nicholas has been a popular dog show judge, officiating at prestigious events throughout the United States and Canada. She is presently approved for all Hounds, all Terriers, all Toys and all Non-Sporting; plus all Pointers, English and Gordon Setters, Vizslas, Weimaraners, and Wirehaired Pointing Griffons in the Sporting Group and Boxers and Dobermans in Working.

In 1970 she became only the third woman ever to have judged Best in Show at the famous Westminster Kennel Club event at Madison Square Garden in New York City, where she has officiated as well on some sixteen other occasions over the years. She has also officiated at such events as Santa Barbara, Chicago International, Morris and Essex, Trenton, Westchester, etc., in the United States; the Sportsman's and the Metropolitan among numerous others in Canada; and Specialty shows in several dozen breeds in both countries. She has judged in almost every one of the United States and in four of the Canadian Provinces. Her dislike of air travel has caused her to refrain from acceptance of constant invitations to officiate in other parts of the world.

Origin and Early History

Among the more popular, attractive and admired "products of Scotland" there is a family of small, unique white dogs who are known as West Highland White Terriers and called, more familiarly, Westies by their friends. These fellows are one of a clan of hardy little workmen whose distinctive appearances separate one from the other, although they share some strongly similar traits and personalities.

The forebears and progenitors of these small canines have included some of the most spirited and useful working terriers who earned respect in former days by their workmanlike abilities, fearlessness, strength and tenacity. To their early owners, they were invaluable for taking badger, fox and otters as well as smaller rodents from the difficult rocky terrain.

Each of these related terrier breeds differed from the others in appearance, yet shared the mutual

From England in the 1930s are three gallant hunters and their "bag", all caught in one night! The West Highland Whites are mother and daughter owned by Miss Ranford. The trio accounted for 101 rodents in just six rat-filled nighttime outings.

characteristics of small size and shortness of leg. They were referred to generally in the beginning as Scotch Terriers to indicate that they were indigenous to Scotland. They were not the Scottish Terriers as we know that breed today, differing sharply in head properties and other characteristics, although they did figure into the Scottie's development.

Each clan of little terriers had its own special characteristics, principally noticed in head properties, length of the body, leg height and general proportions, color and coat quality, right on down to the tail.

The Scotch Terriers of the nineteenth century and earlier provided the ingredients in one form or combination for the eventual emerging of distinctive breeds of dog: such attractive purebreds as the Cairn

11

Terrier and the Westie, so similar to one another except in color; the Skye Terrier with his long body, flaring or drop ears, and lank coat; the Dandie Dinmont Terrier with his big, strong head, domed forehead, full expressive eyes and crisp-feeling coat; and the Scottie with his long and quite narrow classic head and well-muscled compact build.

Obviously the closest resemblance exists between the Cairn and the West Highland White Terri-

ness. The strength of their determination can be felt in the breed's modern-day name of West Highland *White* Terrier.

It is difficult to understand why the Cairn people originally viewed any white touches on their dogs with such extreme distaste; but they did. A puppy Cairn who was white or carried white markings was considered a disgrace to that person's bloodline, and the puppy was culled at birth.

Two early Westies owned by Colonel Malcolm: they are "Sonny" and "Sarah".

It is interesting to note that the white "earth terriers," as they then were frequently referred to, were discovered and admired by French royalty to the extent that, upon learning of their existence, the intrigued James I promptly contacted Argyllshire for "six white earth terriers."

ers, with the most obvious difference being that of color. Separation of color in these two breeds was cultivated with utmost care. The folks raising Cairns wanted theirs to be entirely free of *all* white hair, even on the chest and toes; while those with the dogs who later became West Highlands expected them to be truly *white* terriers, the whiter the better with no traces of tan or yellow—nothing to interfere with the pristine quality of white-

Two people who lived during the turn of the century are credited with advancing development of what is considered the correct Westie type. First place for service to the breed belongs to Colonel E. D. Malcolm, the middle generation of three generations of sponsors of the white earth terriers, his father having been an ardent enthusiast, and his son would follow in the footsteps of his father and grandfather. Colonel Malcolm took the most positive action in developing and popularizing his favorite dog.

Secondly there was, in this same period, the Duke of Argyll. Both of these gentlemen named their strain of white terriers after their estates, thus Col. Malcolm's were called Poltalloch Terriers and The Duke of Argyll's, Roseneath Terriers.

The Poltallochs were the older strain, having been on the Poltalloch estate since about the year 1850. The two strains were not an acceptable color in Skye Terriers any more than in Cairns. We would assume, however, that as the Duke of Argyll became famous for outstanding Skye Terriers under his Roseneath name, that either he succeeded in breeding out the white or that perhaps the dogs were actually pale cream.

In 1903, as interest in and popularity of the white ground terriers started to escalate, it occurred to Colonel Malcolm that a sensible

Eleven West Highland White Terriers from Scotland. Bred by Colonel Malcolm of Poltalloch. Photo by C. Ried, Wishaw.

similar in type, although claimed to be not actually related to each other. The author, however, has read reference to the "Poltalloch-Roseneath Terrier" in designating some small white ground terriers of this general period, so perhaps an interbreeding or two was arranged and experimented with at some point in time.

The Duke of Argyll habitually referred to his terriers as "White Skye Terriers." White, we might add, is breed identification should be bestowed upon them, one descriptive of the dogs themselves, their place of origination and development, and their type of dog. West Highland White Terrier seemed a suitable title for this purpose, and so the new name was made official, and classes for West Highland White Terriers were provided at Crufts in 1907.

Thus, the Westies were on their way!

Coming of Age in England

When, during the year 1860 a dog show held in Birmingham for the first time included terriers in its classification, Scotch Terriers were among them and a "White Skye" was a winner.

Then during 1899, as the famed for West Highland White Terriers was sponsored by the Scottish Kennel Club. In October 1905, again under sponsorship of the Scottish Kennel Club, a seven-and-a-half-month-old puppy won the Championship Certificate in his breed. This

From the days of Scotch Terriers, three Whites among Mr. A.G. Cowley's Scottish Terriers.

Crystal Palace Show held its closing event for that century, an apparently nameless puppy identified only as a "White Scotch Terrier" was among the winners. Although itself nameless, this puppy listed a sire and a dam, White Victor and White Heather respectively in its entry form. The exhibitor was Lady Forbes. Additionally, that same year, a team of Roseneath Terriers belonging to a Dr. Flaxman were among the exhibits here.

Appropriately, the first show anywhere providing separate classes was a little Westie named Morvan, and two years later he became the first "Champion of Record" West Highland White Terrier. Sired by Brogach from Callaig, Champion Morvan was owned by Colin Young.

By 1907, no less than three Westies gained Championship titles, these including Morvan along with one of his offspring, Champion Cromar Snowflake (ex a bitch named Snowdrift), and Champion Oransay, by Conas ex Jean. Snowflake and Oransay both belonged to the Countess of Aberdeen. During the pre-World

War I period of 1907-1916, a total of 27 Westies achieved championship honors.

At this stage in their development, Westies were fortunate in the dedication and support of some very talented, knowledgeable and dedicated breeders. The latter included the famed terrier expert Holland Buckley and his daughter with whom he shared the Westie interest under the identification Scotia Kennels. Another notable fancier was Mrs. B. Lucas who ac-

Two Champions from the famous Wolvey Kennels, owned by Mrs. C. Pacey. *From left to right:* **Ch. Wolvey Peacock** bred by Mrs. E. M. Garnett and **Ch. Wolvey Post,** son of Ch. Wolvey Poacher.

complished good things within the breed. Also this is true of Mrs. M. A. Logan, Mrs. P. Birkin, and several other fanciers like Mrs. Lionel Portman and the lady who owned the Childwicks, Miss Viccars.

Without question, the lion's share of credit for Westie achievement and the breed's advancement to the quality we know today must be bestowed upon that very famous lady Mrs. Cyril Pacey, who brought to the Westie world the legendary "Wolveys." Mrs. Pacey's involvement

with the breeding and exhibiting of West Highland White Terriers started in the years prior to World War I continuing for some 50 accomplishment-filled years until she passed away in 1963.

What can one add to all that has been written over the years on the subject of the Wolveys and their owner? They contributed overwhelmingly to the correct type and quality of the dogs. Mrs. Pacey's vast knowledge of her subject made her an outstanding authority on all

Westie subjects. She sent dogs to wherever the breed was known and to wherever a desire to raise the best existed. It speaks for itself that at the time of her death more than 60 Wolvey champions were on the roster. Pedigree buffs who enjoy researching their dogs' bloodlines back over the generations find the "Wolveys" behind an amazing number of top winners, and the influence of this great line can still be noted in current Westies, despite the fact that Mrs. Pacey has been gone from us now for many years.

It was in 1911 that the first Wolvey to earn a championship was born. Champion Wolvey Piper was bred by Mrs. McLeod, who lived on the Isle of Skye; his parents were Ensar and Culloch. Piper completed his title at age five years. Shortly thereafter and during that same year Champion Wolvey Rhoda joined him on the list of champions.

Westies were getting underway in a thoroughly satisfactory manner when World War I developed, bringing all dog breeding and exhibiting to a halt in Great Britain.

Upon the resumption of peaceful times, the year 1919 found the folks who had waited patiently to resume progress all set to go. One-hundred twenty-six Westie registrations were recorded in that 12 months (which almost doubled in numbers the following year). The first five post-World War I champions in the Westie breed were Charming of Childwick, Highclere Ralet and Highclere Romp, White

Champions from the famous Wolvey Kennels owned by Mrs. C. Pacey. *From left to right:* **Ch. Dawney Busybody** bred by Mrs. L. E. Town in 1923 and **Ch. Wolvey Patrol** bred by Mrs. Pacey in the following year.

Sylph and Wolvey Skylark; their owners, C. Viccars, Mrs. Lucas (two), J. H. Railton, and Mrs. Pacey.

Between 1920 and 1939 (the outbreak of World War II), a total of 125 Westie championships were earned, of which about one-quarter were by Wolvey dogs, led by Champion Wolvey Patrician with an imposing assortment of Best in Show victories to his credit. Patrician also was a very outstanding sire, producing such dogs as Miss Smith-Wood's famed International Champion Ray of Rushmoor and Rodrick of Rushmoor, and also Mrs. Hewson's Clint Crofter who was generally conceded to be the finest of all the many famous Clint-prefixed Westies.

It was in 1936 that Champion Wolvey Pintail was born. She would become one of the most widely admired show bitches of her day.

World War II broke out in 1939. Again the dog shows in Great Britain ceased. However, breeding was not forbidden as it had been during World War I, which was something of a plus from the fancy's point of view since it meant that those who could manage to do so, in the face of unavailability of food along with other problems, did have the option of keeping some dogs over that period. Upon the end of the War, those folks who had kept even a dog or two found themselves with a head start for the future.

Mrs. Inness's fine champion **Ch. Brean Glunyieman.** Photo by R. Robinson.

Among the breeders with this advantage was Mrs. S. Mary Dennis who had written an excellent British publication on the West Highland White Terrier and who owned the Branston Westies. Her Belinda of Branston, who was born in 1937, was the foundation bitch for future generations and produced her first

Ch. Placemore Prosperity owned by Mrs. Allow. Photo by R. Robinson.

From left to right: **Whitebeam Tweedledum** and **Whitebeam Ana** belong to the Hon. Sybil Hood, who was a great early British enthusiast for the West Highland Terrier breed. Photo by R. Robinson.

Challenge Certificates that day to Timochenko of the Roe in dogs and to Macairns Kemima in bitches. Their owners were the Honorable Torfrida Rollo and Mr. Charles Drake, respectively, each owner was winning a C.C. for the first time. In fact, in Mr. Drake's case, it also was his first dog show.

Other early post-World War II Certificate winners included, during August 1947, Mrs. Beel's Freshney Andy who, although the victim of an accident at an early age, nonetheless during his too-short lifetime sired half a dozen champions, among them Champion Athos of Whitehilles, Champion Binnie of Branston, and Champion Cruben Crystal.

The first West Highland White Terrier to become a champion following World War II was in 1947, a bitch named Freshney Fiametta, daughter of Melbourne Mathias who had also sired Freshney Andy.

Fiametta became a Best in Show winner at the Cambridge Championship Show over all breeds, plus gained six Challenge Certificates and six times Best of Breed.

Other new breeders continued to

litters by Bobby of Branston and by Champion Clint Cyrus. Her last litter was by Mrs. Beel's Freshney Andy (Champion Melbourne Mathias ex Freshney Crystal) in which Champion Binnie of Branston was produced in 1949.

The year 1946 saw the post-War re-scheduling of championship shows in Great Britain. A joyous occasion for all English dog folk! In the beginning it was only the specialty shows that were permitted to award championship cards. A splendid sign of the fancy's enthusiasm occurred in the form of 225 Westies entered, a record for the West Highland White Terrier Club of England, at the specialty in Peterborough on July 11, 1946. This was the actual start of the new era. The esteemed judge Winnie Barbour awarded make their presence felt. One who had considerable impact on the Westie world was Mrs. Finch, who racked up an imposing list of honors with Champion Shiningcliff Simon, who not only made up his title with ease but also won Best Terrier at Crufts in 1950 and followed a few weeks later by winning Best in Show at the Scottish Kennel Club in Glasgow. He was equally proficient as a sire with several beautiful champions to his credit.

The big all-breed championship dog shows resumed their post-World War II activities with the event of the East of England Ladies Kennel Association in May 1947 at Petersborough. Mrs. Finch took the dog Shiningcliff Simon to his C.C., and on to his title at Leicester later in the year, when he gained his third C.C. at Glasgow.

In researching the days of the late 1940s into the early 1950s, it becomes abundantly clear that the most successful sire of the period was Furzefield Piper, who never completed his title in the show ring owing to his feistiness and the fact that he had some missing teeth as the aftermath of a kennel fight. He did, however, more than make up for a mere title by the quality of his offspring, who included Miss E. E. Wade's Champion Hookwood Mentor and D. Mary Dennis's Champion Barrister of Branston, who sired 11 champions plus several others with two certificates—the total of which provided an excellent boost to breed quality.

Mrs. Dennis also speaks with pride of her first champion who was the daughter of Freshney Frinton from Baroness of Branston.

International Champion Cruben Dextor was a son of Champion Hookwood Mentor from American Champion Cruben Melphis Chloe. Dextor came to America to the Wishing Well Kennels in 1954, where he became an asset of inestimable value not only to Barbara Kennan but to

Mrs. Cyril Pacey was the best known breeder of West Highland Whites in England in the early period. Here is a group of her famous "Wolveys", showing nice consistency. Photo by Fall.

the entire Westie world of the United States and Canada.

A widely admired and very famous kennel on both sides of the Atlantic is Purston, owned by Michael Colline in Lancaster, England. His fabulously successful Best in Show dogs are Champions Purston Pinmoney Pedlar, Pinmoney Puck, Highlands Angus, Purston Polly Perkins, Ardenrun Andsome of Purston, Purston Primate, Purston Seamate, Purston

called, had been running neck and neck with a beautiful Whippet in competition for England's Top Dog All-Breeds for 1989.

It was close, but when the chips were down, Paddy was Reserve for that honor (Reserve Top Dog of the Year in England is really not at all bad, though.) Then came the Holidays, the New Year 1990, and Crufts! The Whippet was there, too, but this one was Paddy's, and he left there 1990's Best in Show Crufts' Winner

"Black and White"—Times gone by! Westies occurring in Scottie litters today!—perish the thought. Earlier this century this was quite commonplace.

Merrymick, and more. Not to mention the array of Purstons who may never have made it to Best in Show but still do have some good credits in the breed and group competition around the world.

The modern-day British "star" representing a phenomenally successful breeder is Champion Olac Moon Pilot, owned and bred by Derek Tattersall, who also handled this dog to his show triumphs. All during 1989, "Paddy," as Moon Pilot is

over an entry of spectacular quality and size. So, at the 1990 edition of Crufts, the little Westie gained his tenth Championship Best in Show, already having to his credit six times Reserve Best in Show and Top Westie in England for 1987 and 1988.

In reading our kennel stories, you will note that there are Olac Westies of great quality in the United States and Canada exported from this famed kennel.

Early Days in the U.S.A.

West Highland White Terriers were the twelfth Terrier breed to gain admittance to the Stud Book of the American Kennel Club. The first of the breed registered was named Talloch, assigned #115976 during 1908, and belonging to Mrs. Clinton E. Bell of Springfield, Massachusetts.

The next year, 1909, proved to be an important one for West Highlanders as the first A.K.C. Champion of Record was crowned—a British import, Cream of the Skies, #124682. Additionally, the West Highland White Terrier Club of America was first organized under the leadership of fourteen members consisting of an entirely East Coast membership from Connecticut, New Jersey and New York. Approval for the new organization was received without delay, making the West Highland White Terrier Club of America officially an A.K.C. member club as of September 21, 1909. The WHWTCA remains the parent club for the breed in the United States today, but is now flanked by a goodly number of affiliated and regional clubs in all areas of the country.

On December 21, 1909, the breed standard for Westies, as prepared and approved by the WHWTCA, was officially completed and approved by the American Kennel Club. Basically the dog described was the breed as approved in Great Britain. One notes a bare minimum of change in the standard through the years since its inception. Any alterations have been made dealing with size where considerable latitude had originally been provided with height at withers eight to 12 inches,

This is **Ch. Rannoch Dune Down Beat,** a bitch who made history as a consistent Best in Show winner for the Wigtown Kennels of Mrs. B. G. Frame. Her success during the 1960s was notable indeed under George Ward's handling, which we understand took her to 50 times Best in Show among other honors. Here she is winning a Terrier Group at Packerland K.C. in 1966 under judge James Walker Trullinger.

A historic Canadian Westie, **Am. and Can. Ch. Shipmate's Hannibal** at age 15 years. Bred by Mrs. S.J. Navin, owned by Mrs. Daniell-Jenkins, Kennels of the Rouge, Pickering, Ontario, Hannibal was sired by Roseneath Gay Kilt ex Shipmates Confection. He goes back three generations to the Daniell-Jenkins 1952 breeding to Eng., Am. and Can. Ch. Cruben Dextor. With Dextor strongly in his pedigree, he became the dominant sire in the linebreeding programs of the 1960s and '70s as he sired a total of about 70 litters in Canada and in the U.S., including 18 champions.

for his part in having called some of the early Westies to the attention of American fanciers through the activities of his Glenmore Kennels. Mr. Goulet is credited with having been the first to import the Westie to the United States, some of his especially memorable ones having been Champion Kiltie, Champion Maister of Glenmore, and Champion Rumpus of Glenmore.

Mr. Goulet's little white dogs were, indeed, the "start of something big," as while now 11 inches is considered correct.

Prior to these events, however, the little dogs which became known as West Highland White Terriers had made their debut at Westminster in 1906 where they were classified as Roseneath Terriers, the name by which they were first known in the States.

Considerable credit has been accorded Robert Goulet by canine historians

An important Westie "star" of the 1960s, **Am. and Can. Ch. Danny Boy of the Rouge**, by Am. and Can. Ch. Shipmates Hannibal ex Am. Ch. Lintilloch Moment, was bred by Mrs. Daniell-Jenkins, Kennels of the Rouge, Pickering, Ontario. He made an excellent show winner, plus as a stud dog became the sire of several Am. and Can. champions including a Best in Show winner.

with them he established a good breeding program leading to quality homebreds.

Mrs. Roy Rainey gained fame and increased interest for the breed through her Conejos, home to such dogs as Champion Dunvegan Hero and others of inestimable quality. These two kennels along with Arye, Braewood, Greentree, Knoll and Strathspey were the pioneers who set the foundation for West Highland White Terriers back in the early years of the twentieth century.

The Rosster West Highlands, belonging to Miss Claudia Phelps, over a goodly length of time were known for some splendid winners, these having included Champion Clark's Hill Snooker, and, bearing their owner's own kennel identification, Champion Rosster The De'il, Champion Rosster Rajus, and Champion Rosster Reel among others who gained fame.

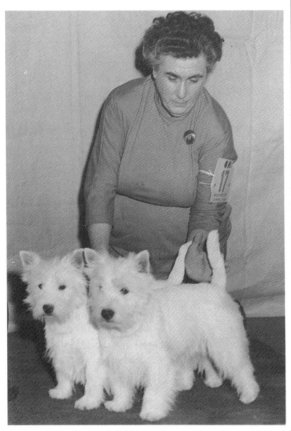

A historic and nostalgic Westminster photo from 1962 of Mrs. Polly Walters winning Best Brace with a pair of her famed Tyndrum Westies. Mrs. Walters was a long-time fancier of this breed who enjoyed the respect and liking of her peers.

Additional well-known American kennels from the early years were Charan, belonging to Captain and Mrs. H. E. H. Chipman, whose dogs were widely acclaimed for their superior quality. Champion Wolvey Pandora of Charan, Champion Wolvey Poet of Charan, Champion Charan Merry Whimsy, and Champion Charan Minstrel were among the headliners here. Minstrel, among his other assets, was a most superb sire who produced an impressive assortment of winners.

Also from the distant past, Nishkenon, owned by Mr. and Mrs. W. R. Rogers was kept to the forefront by such as Champion Nishkenon Scotch Heather and Champion Placemore What Not of Nishkenon.

Mrs. A. B. Monroney has been a member of the West Highland Terrier Club of America for more than 50 years, having joined in 1936. She remains an enthusiastic breeder and exhibitor, never losing interest in her breed of dog.

Above: **Ch. Rainsborowe Redvers** winning Best in Show during the mid-1960s for owner Barbara Worcester Keenan at Baha, Mexico. *Below:* **Am., Can. and Ber. Ch. Symmetra Snip** was the first Westie ever to achieve Best in Show at Montgomery County. Pictured here owner-handled by Barbara Worcester Keenan, Snip is winning another of his prestigious Bests in Show. A very consistent winner, this dog was a Top Ten Westie during the 1960s.

and its parent club, which she served well. She was club president in the 1920s, and a long-time Westie columnist for the A.K.C. *Gazette*. Her kennel identification was Springmeade; among the "greats" who lived there were Champion Ardoch Chief (purchased from Mrs. Rainey); Champion Springmeade Rexminimus; along with his full sister, Champion Springmeade Blackeyed Susan; and their sire, Champion Reaside Rex.

Starting in the late 1920s, there appeared on the scene a breeder destined to become a true trailblazer for Westies. Mrs. John G. Winant, who later became Mrs. Marion Eppley and her Edgerstoune Kennel would help bring the breed to a position not anticipated by even the most enthused Westie advocates.

The death of Miss Marguerite Van Schaich during 1989 took from this breed and from its club, the oldest, most loyal, and devotedly active fancier. For 72 years this lady had been a member of the Westie fancy

In excess of 40 champions emanated from this large and highly successful kennel which thrived through 1954. Some of the more prominent dogs belonging to Mrs. Winant included Champion Ray of

Rushmoor, Champion Clint Casserole, Champion Wolvey Prophet of Edgerstoune, Champion Edgerstoune Radium, Champions Edgerstoune Ringlet, Requa, and Rowdy, and that very famed and wonderful imported bitch Champion Wolvey Pattern of Edgerstoune. It was this latter one who became the first Westie in history to win Best in Show at the Westminster Kennel Club's event in 1942.

Mrs. William Dexter had an early kennel with which to reckon, too. Her kennel known as Heather Hill produced such show dogs as Champions Heather Hill David, Patrick, Peacock, and numerous others.

We have already referred to Champion Wolvey Pattern's breakthrough for the breed being awarded the first Westie Best in Show at the most prestigious dog show in the U.S. known as Westminster. Although this had been far and away the most distinguished honor to date for the little white terriers, credit for early successes must be shared with some other deserving Best in Show winners from this early period. First, Champion Clark's Hill Snooker, owned by Miss Claudia Phelps, won at the Ladies event which was very long ago. And Wolvey Pat-

tern herself did a "dry run" of her Westminster victory by preceding it with similar honors in Manchester, New Hampshire. Still in the 1940s, the American-bred Champion Gillette's Lord Tuffington, belonging to Ben Gillette, gained Best in Show at Hammond, Indiana, in 1944.

Canadian-bred Champion Highland Ursa Major really did himself proud with six Best in Show awards in the United States; Dayton and Indianapolis during 1947 and Savannah, Jacksonville, Des Moines, and Oshkosh, Wisconsin the following year, in 1948.

Owner-handled to Best of Breed at Westminster in 1965, **Ch. Rainsborowe Redvers** was among the notable Westies from Wishing Well Kennels.

Almost simultaneously with Ursa Major was a homebred bitch, Champion Cranbourne Arial, owned by Mrs. John T. Marvin. During 1948, this bitch took the top award at Louisville, following through in 1949 with Bests in Show at Wheeling and Michigan and then Indiana in 1950. After this, Arial really showed off a bit by stepping aside for her daughter, Champion Klintilloch Molly Dee, owned by her co-breeder, Mrs. S. M. Blue. Molly Dee took Best in Show in 1951 at Kokomo, Indiana.

By this time, "Westie fever" was spreading over the entire United States. Additional Westies were stepping into the charmed circle of Best in Show successes and America was becoming increasingly aware of the handsome look of these unique little dogs, their delightful personalities, plus their adaptability to all types of living situations.

So far as winning was concerned, the West Coast had its first Best in Show occasion for the breed when Champion Humby's Dipper gained this award for Almary Henderson at Klamath Falls, Washington, and at Colorado Springs, Colorado.

Champion Cranbourne Atomic, a son of Arial also bred by Mrs. John Marvin, joined Arial's daughter Molly Bee as a Best in Show winner when gaining that award at Lexington, Kentucky, in 1953.

English Champion Cruben Dexter, brought to America by Barbara Worcester Keenan, quickly added the United States and Cana da to his championship territory, stepping into the Best in Show limelight at the big show in Brooklyn, New York. Dexter added to his Best in Show triumphs with several more during 1954, two of which (Canadaigua and Tonawanda in upstate New York) formed the first "back to back" Best in Show victories for a Westie.

On through the

From the 1950s, this is the great-grandsire of the mighty Ch. Elfinbrook Simon, **Ch. Tulyar of Trenean** who, like Simon, was to be found at Wishing Well Kennels among an impressive assortment of Best in Show dogs.

1950s came more Westie success stories. Barbara Keenan added Champion Cruben Flash and Champion Tulyar of Trenean to those from Wishing Well Kennels who belonged to the "Best in Show headliners," among the magnificent Westie quality to be found there. These two achieved the coveted top awards at events in North Carolina and New York respectively. But soon even greater achievements would follow for this kennel!

Mrs. John Marvin achieved a proud record as a breeder during the 1950s when three of her homebreds gained Best in Show distinctions. In addition to Arial and Molly Dee, the third winner was Champion Cranbourne Alexandrite who gained Best in Show for the third and fourth time in 1955.

Both Bea and John Marvin have been great friends to Westies—Bea

Head study of the famed **Ch. Elfinbrook Simon,** an outstanding example of correct Westie type from the early sixties, Simon was Best in Show at Westminster in 1962. Wishing Well Kennels was the proud owner. Photo by Gili.

as a breeder and John as a most authoritative writer, and both of them as exceptional judges. Since his death, John has been sadly missed by all who knew him. We are happy, however, that Bea retains her interest and, although no longer breeding, showing or judging, is seen

Westminster 1964. Barbara Keenan taking Best of Breed with her well-known **Ch. Whitebriar Journeyman.**

and New York area.

And so the foundation was set for the breed and the progress it has attained. The years 1960-1990 have seen the fruit of the earlier foundation. Some fabulous dogs have been shown, and have won in a manner never dreamed possible during early times, and have achieved full recognition for their accomplishments.

visiting with friends and catching up on the Westie news at her favorite dog shows in the Pennsylvania

Ch. Whitebriar Janbaki finishing at Seattle in 1965 at age 18 months. Barbara Keenan, owner, Wishing Well Kennels. Handled by Henry J. Sayres.

During this 30-year period, the Westie has settled firmly and comfortably into a position of stability in the American world of purebred dogs. To all the great breeders and other fanciers who have contributed to this state of affairs, we wish to pay our respects and extend acknowl-edgement of "a job well done."

Florence Worcester and her daughter, who became Barbara Keenan, started a West Highland White Terrier kennel known as Wishing Well back when Barbara was just a youngster. And, as the saying goes, the rest is history. Wishing Well has imported, purchased, owned and bred a collection of West Highlands which immediately put the owners on the map in dog show circles. And to this very day, Barbara and her teenage daughter Patti continue to carry it on, but nowadays with Beagles

An outstanding moment in West Highland White Terrier history, **Ch. Elfinbrook Simon** owned by Wishing Well Kennels, for whom George Ward is handling, winning Best in Show at the Westminster K.C. in 1962, one of only two Westies to date who have received this honor. William A. Rockefeller is presenting the trophy; Heywood Hartley is the judge.

which are Patti's favorites and a breed that Barbara has also owned since childhood.

So far as Westies are concerned, Barbara owned the English-imported Champion Symmetra Snip, who was the first Westie to win Best in Show at Montgomery County in 1960. Sired by Symmetra Skirmish from Symmetra Serener, Snip was bred by B. Taylor and V. Davidson and was born June 27, 1975. His Montgomery victory was under the late and highly respected George Hartman and he was handled by Clifford Hallmark.

By the end of 1960, Snip's show record stood at his having become a multiple Best in Show winner; one of America's Top Ten Terriers for 1960 and '61, plus he was by then the sire of seven champions.

Snip eventually was sold to Goldie Seagraves.

And then along came Simon! Champion Elfinbrook Simon already had some fine Best in Show wins with which he had set a new record on the exciting occasion of his adding Best in Show at Westminster to his laurels. He had won the parent club specialty the previous autumn at Montgomery County, and hopes were high for his success in the breed and even the Terrier Group at Westminster. We are certain that elation must have been at a very high peak when Simon trotted out of the Group ring that day, the blue ribbon clenched tight in the hand of his noted handler, George Ward. Mrs. Worcester and Barbara were barely able to contain their joy a few hours later when Simon again emerged from the ring as the winner—this time the ribbon held in George's hand was for Best in Show!

Presently, only two Westies have been so honored at Westminster. First, Mrs. Winant's splendid Champion Wolvey Pattern of Edgerstoune in 1942; and Champion Elfinbrook Simon exactly two decades later, in 1962. Simon had been born in 1958, bred by Mr. and Mrs. H. Mitchell; was sired by Calluna the Laird from Ichmell Gay Miss.

Mrs. J.H. Daniell-Jenkins with **Sherry Spichip of the Rouge** as a puppy and **Can. Ch. Feolin Dryad of the Rouge.**

Following the Garden (Westminster), Simon proceeded to follow through with some other notable successes, included among them the mighty West Coast classic, Harbor Cities Kennel Club. When he was retired, it was with a total of 27 Bests in Show, a new record for the breed. Another handsome Best in Show dog soon followed at Wishing Well, Champion Whitebriar Journeyman, co-owned by Barbara with Sally Hudson.

Champion Rannoch Dune Down Beat became the next consistent top-winning Westie for owner

An early winner owned by Dr. Hunt. This is **Ch. Highland Angus** handled by Dora Lee Wilson.

Mrs. B. G. Frame. Also handled by George Ward, he began 1966 with a Group second among Terriers at Westminster. He added neatly to his first Best in Show win at Hoosier City when he handily scored four more Bests in Show wins in '66, and then added five more in 1967.

It was during 1967–68 that a handsome dog named Whitebriar Jalisker hit the show rings. Owned by Mr. and Mrs. Herman Fellton and handled by Michele Leathers (now Michele Billings), Jalisker gained the stature which accompanies being a Best in Show winner. This was a time of exceptional quality and activity in Westies, with 90 Terrier Groups and 25 Bests in Show being won by Westies during the period. Wishing Well had a new successful candidate too, Champion Lymehill's Birkfell Solstice.

This is where Champion De Go's Hubert stepped into the picture. A very superior little terrier who lost no time in gaining fame and wide admiration among Westie fanciers and all who judge terriers. De Go Hubert came from a distinguished background, a son of the well-known Best in Show winning Champion Whitebriar Jalisker from Champion Whitebriar Jetstar. He was born on August 14, 1966, bred by Dean Hughes. He was a celebrated sire and his show record was an outstanding series including an impressive number of Terrier Groups and Bests in Show.

Mrs. Jane Esther Henderson, the owner of this wonderful dog, writes to me about Hubert as follows:

The legendary **Ch. De Go's Hubert,** an all-time "great" in the breed, was campaigned during the late 1960s into the early '70s period during which he accounted for a tremendous number of Terrier Groups including the Best in Show at the big Terrier event, Montgomery County, in 1971 and a wide array of Bests in Show. Bred from English imports, "Hollis," as he was known, was selected and purchased by Mrs. Jane Esther Henderson and handled by Clifford Hallmark.

buying something on my own. I telephoned nervously that night and Cliff replied 'Congratulations! He's the best Westie I ever saw'!"

"De Go's Hubert was of Whitebriar background, and he received the award for doing so after siring ten champion get. His show record was almost unequalled, including nearly every major award except Westminster. The year he was entered there he acquired a virus that week and we had to scratch him.

"Hollis, as Hubert always was called, was born in a trailer court in Georgia, and it was I who selected him and brought him after considerable 'wheeler dealing' with his owner. He was shipped to Newark Airport and Cliff Hallmark drove up to fetch him, annoyed at me for

It had been Mrs. Henderson's intention to show Hollis herself, but

Ch. Lymehill's Birkfell Solstice, a Best in Show winner of the late 1960s, handled here to Best in Show by Henry J. Sayres for Wishing Well Kennels.

Ch. Ardenrun Andsome of Purston being congratulated by his handler Dora Lee Wilson, as they sit together on the "victory ramp" where Andy has just been awarded his first Best in Show at Des Moines K.C. in 1974. Dr. Alvaro T. Hunt was the owner of this splendid little dog, a truly unforgettable Westie.

33

as the excitement mounted over his quality and excellence, she realized that she could not adequately campaign him that way, and so she turned him over to Cliff for his show career.

Hollis achieved his tremendous number of Terrier Group awards in keenest Eastern competition and from our most respected judges. Bill Kendrick considered him and the noted Pekingese, Chik Tsun, the two best dogs he ever judged. Comments such as this came from all sides. Truly this little Scotsman, Hollis, had become a legend in his own lifetime.

It was at the 1971 Montgomery County Terrier event, that most prestigious for Terriers, that Hollis—in a veritable sea of mud, so wet had been the weather—scored one of his most treasured double victories by going first Best of Breed in the West Highland Terrier Club of America Specialty under judge Terrence Bresnahan, and then Best in Show under Mrs. Augustus Riggs.

As the 1960s drew to a close, thrilling wins for Westies were escalating. In 1968 alone, six dogs accounted for a total of 25 Bests in Show, led by Champion Rannock Dune Down Beat who had started out so well the previous year for owner Mrs. B. G. Frame and handler George Ward. By the end of '68 he had acquired 11 new listings to the earlier total of around half a dozen or more already acquired.

Am. and Can. Ch. Forest Glen Hannipeg, by Am. and Can. Ch. Shipmates Hannibal ex Am. and Can. Ch. So Eagerly of Forest Glen, is a Group winner from the classes. Bred by Mrs. Clarence Fawcett; owned by Mrs. Daniell-Jenkins, Kennels of the Rouge, Pickering, Ontario, Canada.

Prominent American Westie Kennels

BAYOU GLEN

Bayou Glen West Highland White Terriers, belonging to Dr. Alvaro T. Hunt at New Orleans, Louisiana, has made some exceptionally strong and significant contributions to the success of this breed in the United States.

Champion Highlands Angus was an American-bred winner from this kennel. But in 1974 Dr. Hunt's dogs started REALLY to make a mark on breed history with the importation of the little dog known informally as Andy. Officially Andy was known as English Champion Ardenrun Andsome of Purston, a Westie who carved for himself a niche which will never be forgotten—indeed a Westie of rare distinction.

Andy was a son of Champion Whitebriar Jonfair from Ardenrun Agitator. He was bred by C. Oakley and exported from England to the United States by Reverend Collings, owner of Purston Kennels.

Despite the fact that a portion of 1974 had passed prior to Andy's arrival, and his show debut in the United States, he was well established when that year closed having gained his American championship and various other honors, including eight all-breed Bests in Show. By January 1975 everyone who had heard of his excellence but not yet seen this new prospective record-breaker was eager to do so, and few, if any, were disappointed.

Ch. Ardenrun Andsome of Purston on the occasion of his last Best in Show on the day prior to his retirement, December 1977. Owned by Dr. Alvaro Hunt for whom he was handled to a brilliant career by Dora Lee Wilson.

Andy was campaigned with the fearlessness and abandon befitting his excellent quality. He was placed in the charge of Mrs. Dora Lee Wilson who handled him to his many triumphs.

His first Montgomery show entry was in 1974, where he won the breed under Mrs. James Edward Clark but was unplaced in the Group. The second year he attended Montgomery he came away the Best in Show winner under Heywood Hartley, having gained the breed under Barbara Keenan.

For 1975 Andy amassed sufficient Terrier Group firsts to become the Quaker Oats Award winner as the outstanding winning Terrier in competition that year—these Groups having included Westminsters plus 19 which led to Best in Show, bringing the total Bests in

Ch. Purston Merrymick winning Best in Show at Cedar Rapids in June 1980, handled by Dora Lee Wilson for owner Dr. Alvaro T. Hunt, Bayou Glen Kennels, New Orleans, LA.

Show to 28. Another 11 Bests in Show prior to his retirement during 1976 brought Andy's total count of such victories to 39.

1977 saw Dr. Hunt represented with another Best in Show dog who had also been imported from England, Champion Purston Primate, who won a Best in Show that year and then followed through with an additional five the following year.

After that Champion Purston Merrymick came to Dr. Hunt, also joining the Best in Show winning ranks. Like Andy, both Primate and Merrymick had Montgomery Bests of Breed to their credit, under breeder-judge Bea Marvin and John Ward respectively; both times handled by Mrs. Wilson.

BEL-WEST

The Bel-West Kennels has been active with the West Highland White Terrier since 1977 in Phoenix, Arizona, when owners Harold and Maura Heubel acquired their first Westie show dog. This little bitch, Jasmine, was a daughter of English Champion Ardenrun Andsome of Purston and she ultimately became a champion.

Next, the Heubels imported some other greatly admired British Westies, the first of which was Champion Purston Primemover, known as Evelyn, who was a littermate to Champion Purston Merrymick.

Primemover produced many champions, including a daughter, Bel-West Buttercup, who brought further honors to the family by becoming the dam of 13 champions in

Ch. Olac Moonpenny of Bel-West, by Ch. Olac Mooncopy of Marank ex Eng. Ch. Halfmoon of Olac, is an important figure in the breeding program at Bel-West Kennels, owned by the Harold Heubels at Phoenix, AZ. This photo depicts Penny's first show, in November 1986 where she took Winners Bitch, Best of Winners and Best of Opposite Sex for her first point.

her own right.

Champion Arnholme Applause, co-owned with Jim Saunders, led to three additional importations for Bel-West, all quite closely related to her. They are the basis of Bel-West's current breeding and showing program, the results of which are proving impressively successful.

One of these imported bitches is Champion Olac Moonpenny of Bel-West, the Top Winning Bitch in the United States for 1988 and 1989. She has several Group placements including a Group first; and is a

Best in Specialty Show winner, too. She was also Best of Opposite Sex at Montgomery County in 1989.

Moonpenny is out of Olac Mooncopy of Marank and English Champion Halfmoon of Olac. She was bred by Derek Tattersall.

Champion Bel-West Lace Belle was among the top-winning Westie bitches of 1990. She was Best of Opposite Sex at the Great Western Specialty Show in Southern California, has several Group placements including a Group second; and is one of three champions from

Moonpenny's litter by Champion Mac-Ken-Char's Irish Navigator.

The Heubels take particular pride in their stud dog, both for his own quality and for his family connections. He is a litter brother to the 1990 Crufts' Best in Show dog, English Champion Olac Moonpilot. There are some superlative puppies in the kennel now by Moonblaze, who along with some excellent young bitches make for an exciting future for Bel-West and its owners.

With lots of maturing to do, the future **Am. and Can. Ch. Cloudcroft's Mulberry Punch** wins the 6-9 Month Puppy Class at Montgomery County in October 1989. Five months later this Westie was Group Second among the Terriers at Seattle Kennel Club. Cloudcroft's Mulberry Punch was bred by Gale McDonald, Sutherlin, OR.

CLOUDCROFT

Cloudcroft West Highland White Terriers, at Sutherlin, Oregon, is owned by Gale L. McDonald, a comparatively new breeder who acquired her first Westie in 1981.

It became increasingly evident (as so frequently happens with first purchases) that this original Westie was not of the type she wanted to show or breed. Even though Gale and her husband love the dog dearly as a pet, and consider him the "best dog in the world" (he won Best Puppy in Match at their first attempt to show him), it did not take them long to realize that he did not have the type or quality exhibited by the dogs they were seeing at the shows. He is neutered now but still remains the McDonalds' beloved pet.

Gale realized very quickly that she would need a Westie of such excellent quality that it could overcome her novice handling and grooming. She met Goeff and Mary Charles of the Glenfinnan Kennels in 1982, and upon first seeing their dogs realized instantly that this was the type that she wanted for her own program.

Gale waited a year and a half for a top-quality bitch puppy from Glenfinnan, which turned out to have been time well spent, as this puppy grew up to become Champion Glenfinnan's Proud As Punch, the Cloudcroft foundation bitch. Gale owner-handled Punch to her championship, placing Group second under

Cloudcroft's Punchline, bred and owned by Gale L. McDonald, at age 10 months placing in the Terrier Group. Mrs. McDonald handling.

Mrs. Tom Stevenson on the day she finished. Needless to say, a happy, exciting day for Gale as a then-quite-new Westie fancier.

Since that time, Punch has produced some excellent puppies. One son, Canadian Champion Cloudcroft's Mulberry Punch, out of Champion Glenfinnan's Woo Woo Kid, is now owned by Madeline Kronby of Milton, Canada. He attained his Canadian title before becoming one year old, winning four Canadian Best Puppy in Show awards, has multiple Canadian Group placements; won the 6-9 Month Puppy Class at Montgomery County in 1989; and quickly both of his U.S. "majors." At Seattle in 1990, he was Group second at the Seattle Kennel Club Dog Show.

Another son, Cloudcroft Punchline, out of Champion Sno-

Bilt's Puzzle, retained by the McDonalds for their own kennel, won the Sweepstakes at the Puget Sound West Highland White Terrier Club in 1989; placed Best of Opposite Sex in the Sweepstakes at Montgomery County in 1989; and has a Terrier Group fourth at an all-breed dog show.

COUNTRY

Country is the prefix used by Linda McCutcheon, of Philadelphia, Pennsylvania, to register her excellent Westies, all of whom are descended from a little bitch co-owned by Linda with Dr. W. H. Sterg O'Dell.

This bitch was from the Famecheck strain and was bred to Champion Kemyell Krackerjack owned by Dr. O'Dell.

This mating produced three puppies, two boys and one girl. Linda kept the female while Dr. O'Dell took the two males, one of them

Ch. Country Girl Scooter Pie, by Ch. Kemyell Krackerjack ex Stergo Debbie, has produced five champions for her breeder-owner Linda McCutcheon, Philadelphia, PA.

Ch. Stergo Bronco Billy, by Ch. Kemyell Krackerjack ex Stergo Debbie, was bred by Linda McCutcheon and is owned by Dr. W.H. Sterg O'Dell. Pictured taking Best of Winners, Montgomery County 1982.

going to his son. The other embarked on a show career to become Champion Stergo Bronco Billy with an excellent Best of Winners award at Montgomery 1982 along the way. Linda's puppy bitch from this litter was named Country Girl Scooter Pie and also made her championship in style, her victories having included Winners Bitch at the Ohio West Highland Club Specialty 1983 and Best of Opposite Sex at the Baltimore Specialty in 1985. Champion Country Girl Scooter Pie was rarely "specialed," but she did win the Veteran's for bitches at Montgomery County at age seven years.

After gaining her title, Scooter Pie was bred to American, Bermudan, Canadian Champion Mac-Ken-Char's Irish Navigator. From this she produced four champions who, added to her one earlier Champion Daniel Stergo Disco Dancer (by Famecheck Daniel), brought her total to five, making her eligible for the West Highland White Terrier Club's Brood Bitch award for 1989.

The four champions in the Scooter Pie–Irish Navigator litter are as follows:

Champion Country Boy Irish Rouge; Champion Country Boy Irish Shawnnesy, a winner in Group and Sweepstakes competition; Champion Country Girl Irish Brandy, a specialty winner; and Champion Country Girl Irish Emerald.

Mrs. McCutcheon comments: "Scooter Pie's dam was predominantly Famecheck and her sire was Whitebriar. It was one of those breedings that 'clicked,' as did the Scooter Pie–Navigator breedings. Most of these champions were owner-handled, Brandy from the Bred-by Exhibitor Class. Margery Good helped to finish the dogs in the early years, until Mrs. McCutcheon could master the art of grooming to compete with the handlers. It has been most gratifying!"

DALRIADA

Dalriada West Highland White Terriers in Fairfax, Virginia, is the result of owner Janis Chapman's having been introduced to the breed when she lived in London, England, more than 20 years ago. Everyone there had one of these cute white dogs, and soon so did Janis.

When she returned to the United States in 1972, she was accompanied by a dog she had purchased from an unknown kitchen breeder located in the Mid-

lands, and a puppy bitch from the well-known breeder Mrs. Pritchard of Melwyn fame.

Encouraged by a lady who later was to become her best friend, Janis became involved in showing as well as breeding her Westie bitch. After a reasonable length of time, her dog Champion Clyde of Creag Meagaidh completed his title, following which Dalriada came into existence.

This kennel has always been a hobby for its owner, with a population not exceeding eight or nine dogs. Usually there has been a litter about once a year.

As with many other hobbyists, there came a time when it was necessary to start over. Janis's friend Kathleen Kurdziolek enabled her to do this by the gift of a lovely bitch of her breeding from which Janis made

Ch. Clyde of Creag Meagaidh, by Macleod of Knockinelder ex Mandy Roberts. Ms. Janis Chapman, owner, Dalriada Kennels, Fairfax, VA.

a new beginning. That bitch, Happiness Is Rowdee, who incidentally hated dog shows, is behind everything on which Dalriada is built.

Champion Dalriada Sam I Am is described by Ms. Chapman as the "culmination of my breeding plan, and the only *big* winner I have had. I hope that he makes as big an impact on the breed as he should, because he is so correct." Sam finished his championship in February 1989. As a "special" he has captured nearly 40 Bests of Breed, has won seven Terrier Groups, plus numerous Group placements. He also is a specialty show winner.

That handsome little showman **Ch. Dalriada Sam I Am** winning the breed from the author at Langley K.C. in 1990. Bill Kamai handling for breeder-owner Janis Chapman, Fairfax, Virginia. Sam has many Terrier Group firsts to his credit.

intelligent little dogs.

American, Canadian Champion Royal Scott's Lady Abigail, American, Canadian C.D., who also has earned a Certificate of Gameness, is the foundation of all Dawn's Westies. Among her accomplishments are winning both obedience awards offered by the national club during her bid for her Companion Dog degree in 1982. She also captured the Versatility Award by her willingness to work at all endeavors. Through her son, Adam, and her daughter, Sara (both sired by International Champion Skaket's Candy Man, C.D.X., T.D., C.G.) have come several specialty and sweepstakes winners, champions, and the future generations of Dawn's Highland Scots. Abby's sire is American, Canadian Champion Mac-Ken-Chars Number Onederful. Her dam is Champion Rouge Noelles Eminent Naomi. Both are linebred

DAWN'S
HIGHLAND SCOTS

Dawn's Highland Scots are owned by Dawn L. Martin of Saylorsburg, Pennsylvania, who has been active with her Westies since 1979, participating in conformation competition, obedience, versatility and gameness with her handsome and descendents of International Champion Cruben Dextor.

American and Canadian Champion Dawn's Up 'N' Adam, American, Canadian C.D.X., C.G., is Abby's best known son. He is a Best in Show winner in Canada, and a Group winner in the United States. While earning his Companion Dog status in Canada in 1984, Adam received a score of 197, a first place, and a fourth place. In 1985 the Martins returned to Canada where Adam gained his Companion Dog Excellent degree, which included a tie for first place. In 1986 Adam received his American Companion Dog degree with a class placement and several Highest Scoring Terrier in Trial awards. Adam also excels at hunting, and holds the Versatility Award title. His son, Dawn's Bright 'N' Early, C.D., known as "Piper," is a High in Trial winner. Piper is owned by Margaret Schrader.

American and Canadian Champion Dawn's Rise 'N' Shine (Casey) was sired by Champion Briarton Pete of Stonecourt ex Dawn's Sunshine Sara, and is the mother of the Best in Show Brace which attracted tremendous admiration at Montgomery County in 1989. The duo was handled by 12-year-old Jonathan Marks, Jr. Casey was the recipient of the Bred-by-Exhibitor award from the national club while accumulating all her championship points from the Bred-by-Exhibitor Class. Casey's face, incidentally, enhances the front of the Nabisco Milk Bone Dog Treat® package.

All of the Westies at Dawn's are Therapy Dogs and regular visitors to the local nursing homes.

Adam has been making friends among the students at the local junior high school where careers in

Am. and Can. Ch. Royal Scott's Lady Abigail, Am. and Can. C.D., C.G. By Am. and Can. Ch. Mac-Ken-Char's Number Onederful ex Am. Ch. Rouge Noelles Eminent Naomi. Breeder, Roy O. Wuchter, Sr. Owner, Dawn L. Martin, Dawn's Highland Scots, Saylorsville, PA.

animals are discussed by Dawn and others. Adam, like the show-off that he is, has a marvelous time honking a bicycle horn in response to hand

Best in Show **Am. and Can. Ch. Dawn's Up "N" Adam, Am. and Can. C.D.X., C.G**. by FCI Int. Am., Can., Mex., and Ber. Ch. Skaket's Candy Man, C.D.X., T.D., C.G. ex Am. and Can. Ch. Royal Scott's Lady Abigail, Am. and Can. C.D., C.G. Breeder-owner, Dawn L. Martin, Saylorsburg, PA.

signals, and barking when shown the grate over the heat ducts where he is told there is a rat! All in all, a very clever little fellow who finds life to be full of many interesting things though he has retired from the show ring!

GARDNER

Gardner West Highland White Terriers is in Closter, New Jersey, where they are owned by Carolyn Gardner. Carolyn became involved with this breed when she bought one as a pet for her son. This bitch was a daughter of Champion Braidholme White Tornado of Binate and a granddaughter of Champion Prosswick's Persuas. In addition to bringing pleasure as a pet, she became Champion Macskathll's Lady Harrison and the foundation bitch for Gardner Westies.

Lady Harrison joined the Gardner family in 1980. In due course she was bred to Champion Cynosure Orion the Hunter, who also was descended from Prosswick's

Persuas. They produced Champion Gardner's Morning Glory, who was Mrs. Gardner's first homebred champion, gaining her title in 1981. Carolyn later bought her foundation dog, "Murray" a.k.a. American, Canadian Champion Gardner's Frost Bud o' Mauradoon, whose pedigree goes back five times to International Champion Monsieur Aus Der Flerlage. Murray was a specialty winner and was finished by Carolyn prior to reaching the age of 18 months. He then went on to gain his Canadian championship in one four-show weekend, taking good placements each day.

She continued to outcross to incorporate these lines, and then later brought in some of the Irish Navigator line.

There are now several homebred owner-handled champions, one of the most recent being a Group-placing bitch Champion Gardner's Blk Eye Susan Orion, co-owned by Carolyn with Orion Westies. This lovely bitch finished for her owner-

handler with three "majors", two Bests of Breed, and a Group second from the classes. She was later bred to Best in Show Champion Sno Bites Puzzle, a complete outcross for Gardner Westies.

This is a small, home-type kennel whose owner does all her own grooming and showing. She also has judged a few matches as well as the New York Sweepstakes.

Ch. Gardner's Morning Glory, Carolyn Gardner's first homebred champion, winning a "major" from the puppy classes, owner-handled. Morning Glory was also Best of Opposite Sex in Sweepstakes at the Roving Specialty during 1981 in Plainfield, NJ.

GLENGIDGE

Glengidge West Highland White Terriers belongs to Helene and Seymour Weiss at Brooklyn, New York.

It was in the summer of 1966 when Miss Helene Andrews purchased her first West Highland White

Terrier as a pet, never thinking then that her new puppy would be the passport to a hitherto undreamed-of lifestyle. The puppy grew up to be Rosent's Jeannette, dam of the first Glengidge champion, and a constant friend and confidant for almost 18 years.

As things developed, Miss Andrews decided to learn how good

champion, who was a dog, Champion Glengidge Precocious, and who was sired by Champion Bev-Vic's Gallant Duncan.

By the time the first Glengidge championship was earned, Miss Andrews had met and married Seymour Weiss, a well-known terrier man. Together, the Weisses set about establishing a family of fine Westies that would be a credit to the breed and to their breeders.

As a result of repeated whelping and mortality problems, the Weisses decided to make a new start in their breeding program. The aim for quality remained the same, but the effort was to breed from a family that was hopefully free of the problems that plagued the Glengidges up to that time.

The Weisses purchased a puppy from Mr. and Mrs. John T. Ward that would provide this foundation. The puppy grew up

Ch. Glengidge Precocious, by Ch. Bev-Vic's Gallant Duncan ex Rosent's Jeannette, is the first of the Glengidge champions owned by Helene and Seymour Weiss.

her pet really was, and thus made the acquaintance of a number of handlers and owners at shows in both New Jersey and southern Florida. As a result, her first Westie, who was a granddaughter of Champion Famecheck Viking, was never entered in the ring but was bred and became the dam of Helene's first

to become Champion Donnybrook's Eve, by Champion Donnybrook's Benjamin ex Champion Whitebriar Jolyminx. Ironically Eve produced only one litter in her lifetime despite repeated efforts. Nonetheless that one litter was sired by the immortal great, English Champion Pillerton Peterman. From the "crime" litter, the Weisses retained a brother and a sister who were to become Champion Glengidge Pickpocket and Champion Glengidge Easy Virtue. The Weisses accredit the power of good line-breeding and the quality of these two siblings for the real success of the Glengidge family. When the daughters of Easy Virtue were bred to their uncle, the results were Westies of quality that proved that they could win and produce.

Ch. Glengidge Easy Virtue, by Ch. Pillerton Peterman ex Ch. Donnybrook's Eve, was Best of Winners at Westminster K.C. in 1976, under judge Dr. Josephine Deubler, Seymour Weiss handling for himself and co-owner Helene Weiss of Glengidge Westies, Brooklyn, NY.

Easy Virtue was sent to be bred to the outstanding winner and producer Alvaro Hunt's Champion Ardenrun Andsome of Purston, thus the Weisses got two good producers, Champion Glengidge Candy Kiss and Glengidge Ultra Violet, full sisters from different litters. Candy Kiss, bred to Wishing Well Kennels' Champion Kristajen Crackerjack, produced Champion Glengidge Birthday Promise; and bred to her uncle Pickpocket, produced the strong winner and producer Champion Glengidge Plum Candy. Ultra Violet never finished but produced a winner and producer in Champion Glengidge Tabitha Twitchett, also by Pickpocket.

There was yet another from Easy Virtue that was a great favorite of many. She was the daughter of Champion Biljonblue's Bee Gee, her name Champion Glengidge Ultimate Violet. A Sweepstakes winner and champion from the Bred-by-Exhibitor Class, she sadly never had a litter for her breeders.

The aforementioned Twitch and Plum Candy brought great strength to the Glengidge breeding program. Twitch was bred three times to the celebrated Champion Mac-Ken-Char's Irish Navigator, and this combination proved to be a good one with a number of exciting results. Plus Candy and Twitch were cousins, but on paper could have been sisters; and Plum Candy also proved a good nick with Navigator, producing some of Glengidge's best Westies to date.

Every family that uses linebreeding needs to go out at times to introduce fresh genetic patterns, and to this end the Weisses imported Champion Whitebriar Jaymandie in 1978. Like "Eve," "J.J." was to produce only one litter, and this was by the foundation stud, Pickpocket. This mating produced no champions, but was noteworthy in that the bitch, Glengidge Giggles, when bred to Irish Navigator produced the Group and Specialty winner Champion Glengidge Happy

Ch. Glengidge Candy Kiss, by Ch. Ardenrun Andsome of Purston ex Ch. Glengidge Easy Virtue, Winners Bitch at the West Highland White Terrier Club of Greater Washington under breeder-judge Barbara Keenan. Guenter Behr handling for owners Helene and Seymour Weiss, Brooklyn, NY.

Hooligan and also Champion Glengidge Happy Hooker, plus from a mating to Champion Whitebriar Jeronimo came Champion Glengidge Kate in the Kitchen.

There have been some twenty Glengidge champions since 1975, including such standouts as Champion Glengidge Moxie Mac-Ken-Char, Champion Glengidge Ladyhawke, Champion Glengidge Social Climber, and Champion Glengidge Social Butterfly, presently all with other owners.

Helene and Seymour Weiss are great believers in the role of the breeder and the importance of the Bred-by-Exhibitor Class in the West Highland breed. They have set a pattern and example for others in actively supporting the class themselves, and have finished no fewer than seven from Bred-by exclusively, with others scoring at least some of their points from this breeders' class.

The latest star from this kennel is really blowing up a storm. This is Ch. Glengidge Golden Charm, bred by the Weisses, owned by Helene Weiss and Judy Lewis, handled by Lanny Hirstein. A sensation in the Sweepstakes at Montgomery as a puppy, she came on like gangbusters and is now enjoying a lively career as a Group winner.

HOLYROOD

Holyrood Westies, in Unionville, Connecticut, began in 1979 when Judy Francisco purchased her foundation bitch from Muriel Whitman in Troy, New York.

Mrs. Whitman had bred a bitch she bought from Patty Storey to a lovely male belonging to Ann Frinks. These two Westies were Champion Lonsdale Lillith bred to Champion Jeremy of Windy Hill, and they produced the wonderful Champion Whitemount Frolic TWA.

It was Frolic who came to Judy Francisco and served as Holyrood's foundation.

Champion Jeremy of Windy Hill was Top-Winning Westie Puppy Dog in 1978. He is a full brother to the foundation bitch of the Kilkerran Westies, Champion Kortni of Windy Hill.

Frolic was a winner in her own right having been awarded Best Puppy Bitch in Westies for 1980 by the WHWTCA. She was shown to her championship by Roberta Campbell, and was undefeated in the open classes, gaining her title when just 15 months of age.

As a producer, Frolic also did herself proud. She was bred to three stud

The foundation bitch of Holyrood's Westies, **Ch. Whitemount Frolic TWA**, by Ch. Jeremy of Windy Hill ex Ch. Lonsdale Lillith. She was bred by Muriel Whitman, owned by Judith J. Francisco, and handled by Roberta Campbell. Winning points here in 1980 under terrier expert and all-breed judge Thomas Gately.

Ch. Holyrood's Ms. Mayhem, by Ch. Kilkerran the Joker is Wild ex Ch. Whitemount Frolic TWA. Owned by Marilyn Foster and breeder Judith J. Francisco, Unionville, CT, Mayhem is winning Best of Breed on the New England circuit, July 1987.

dogs and produced a total of ten puppies, six of her daughters having also become champions and the others were never shown. They were Champion Holyrood's Hot Toddy, owned by Judy Francisco, a granddam of Champion Principal's MacGyver; Champion Holyrood's Dressed in Plaid and Champion Holyrood's Candy Apple, who were never bred by their owners; Champion Holyrood's Busybody, owned by Donna Williams and Henriette Ruhl, who has many champion offspring and specialty winners; Champion Holyrood's Liza with a Z, owned by Judy Francisco; and Champion Holyrood's Ms. Mayhem, owned by Marilyn Foster and Judy Francisco.

When bred to Champion Glenfinnan's Something Dandy, Ms. Mayhem produced Holyrood's Hootnanny O'Shelly Bay. "Fanny" was Reserve Winners Bitch from the 9–12 Month Puppy Class at Montgomery County in 1988, and was Best in Sweepstakes in the California WHWTC Specialty in 1989, and Best of Opposite Sex in the Sweepstakes at the Trinity Valley Specialty in 1989. She belongs to Dr. Marcia Montgomery and Judy Francisco.

Hootnanny's litter brother Champion Holyrood's Hopscot O'Shelly Bay was Reserve Winners Dog at the Roving Specialty in June 1989 in Pennsylvania, and finished his

Holyrood's Hootnanny O'Shelly Bay, by Ch. Glenfinnan's Something Dandy ex Ch. Holyrood's Ms. Mayhem. Bred by M. Foster and Judith Francisco; owners, Marcia Montgomery, MD., Judith Francisco and M. Foster. Taking Reserve Winners at Montgomery County 1988.

title with four "majors" in Boston, the final one at Ladies Dog Club in Boston the following November. He was shown throughout his career by Judy Francisco and Bernard Sims.

Fannie's other litter brother, Champion Holyrood's Hootman O'Shelly, is a multiple specialty and Best in Show winner. He was Best of Breed at Hatboro, Devon and Montgomery County in 1989 and has five Best in Show victories on his record. He also was Best of Breed at Westminster in both 1989 and 1990. He is owned by Dr. James and Elizabeth Boso.

Litter sister to Ms. Mayhem, Liza with a Z has also spectacular show victories to record. She is the only Westie to be shown only at specialty shows. Shown at six specialties, she won four of them to finish, certainly no small accomplishment when one considers the competition at these events.

Liza with a Z has three promising young sons working on careers and they show every sign of carrying on the family tradition of success.

Judy Francisco relays that her dogs originally descend from Champion Cruben Dextor, combined with what she considers to have been the best of Ruth Birmingham's Lochcrest lines and Katherine Hayward's Huntingtonhouse lines.

KILKERRAN

Kilkerran West Highland White Terriers belongs to Kathy and Wayne Kompare in Danbury, Connecticut, where they have assembled a most outstanding collection of quality

Ch. Kortni of Windy Hill taking Best of Breed at the Greater NY Specialty, Westchester K.C., handled by Roberta Campbell for owners Kathy and Wayne Kompare.

members of this breed.

There is an old saying that a kennel is no better than its bitches, and the longer that one breeds, the more aware one becomes of its truth. The Kompares wanted a linebred bitch for their foundation, and waited three years for Kortni of Windy Hill, who was closely linebred to English and Canadian Champion Cruben Dextor. They were truly lucky in their choice, a fact which, due to inexperience, they did not realize until later.

Kortni turned out to be the progenitor of all the Kompares' success and the dominant background of Kilkerran Westies. Very quickly Kortni proved herself to be a great show bitch. She loved every minute in the ring, and judges were happy to reward her for it. She finished her championship at the Greater New York Westie Specialty, held in conjunction with Westchester Kennel Club by going Best of Breed over 11 "specials." The Kompares started to

Best in Show **Am. and Can. Ch. Kilkerran D'Artagnan,** by Cynosure Orion the Hunter ex Ch. Kortni of Windy HIll, with his handler, Dora Lee Wilson, winning for breeders-owners Kathy and Wayne Kompare.

realize at that point that Kortni's breeder, Ann M. Frinks, had given them something *very* special.

Kortni had that ephemeral and so necessary ingredient of all show dogs known as "charisma." She has passed this along to her puppies, as well as her gorgeous head, beautiful front and shoulders, and short back with correct tail. She became the dam of only nine puppies during her lifetime; but of these nine, six became champions and one was the Kompares' first multiple Best in Show winner, American and Canadian Champion Kilkerran D'Artagnan. Most all of the Kompares' 25+ homebred champions descend from Kortni. She is the granddam of Champion Kilkerran 'N Wicket A Kut Above (Kutter), another multiple Best in Show winner; and great granddam of two other Best in Show dogs. The Kompares attribute this success to Kortni's prepotency and to their policy of linebreeding whenever possible and only outcrossing when needed for a particular trait.

Kilkerran owes a big "thank you" to Nancy Spelke, co-owner and handler of Champion Kilkerran N'Wicket A Kut Above. A novice when she began, Nancy conditioned and handled "Kutter" for two wonderful years during which he earned four Specialty Bests of Breed, and became the Kompares' second multiple Best in Show dog. His record now stands at 137 times Best of Breed, 100 Group placements, the latter including 37 times Best Terrier in Show, plus his many Bests in Show.

A beautifully balanced and handsome Westie. **Ch. Kilkerran 'N Wicket A Kut Above** is owned by his handler Nancy Spelke, his breeder Kathy Kompare, and Laura Moreno.

Success came quickly to Kilkerran, whose first litter in 1981 brought forth the Singleton puppy, the kennel's first champion. As time went on, many friends in the breed proved helpful by contributing to the Kompares' knowledge, and therefore their success as breeders of specialty and sweepstakes winners. The time came for them to return some of the generous assistance from which they had greatly benefitted. Wayne was serving on the board of the national club and then as treasurer for three years in addition to chairing several sweepstakes, including the National at Montgomery County. Kathy has been the subscription co-ordinator for the national publication, "The

Westie Imprint" since that publication's inception, and she has contributed articles to it in addition to serving on committees.

The Kompares look forward to the future. Kortni died in 1988, but she left a legacy that lives on. Champion

Patricia Storey owner-handling her first Westie and first champion to his title. This 1967 event led to the Lonsdale Kennels' establishment and to the Storeys' enthusiasm for the breed. This is **Ch. Westcote Ghillie of Fairloch.**

Kilkerran Name of the Game (known as Fame), a Kortni granddaughter and specialty winner, is proving to be the second foundation bitch in the ring and in the whelping box. Her linebred son, Champion Kilkerran Quintessence, seems destined for a bright future as a "special" and as a producer, which he is already fulfilling with Nancy Spelke as a Best in Show dog.

LONSDALE

The Lonsdale West Highland White Terriers is owned by Patricia Storey and located in New England, at Dedham, Massachusetts. The line started in 1967, when Patricia's first Westie, "Ghillie," completed his title, becoming Champion Westcote Ghillie of Fairloch, he a son of Champion Westcote Highloch.

By the time that this had taken place, the Storeys had become greatly enamored of the breed and of the fun of dog shows. Thus Patricia immediately purchased her first brood matron, this one from Tom and Thelma Adams of the famed Canadian Westie kennel Roseneath. This bitch, Roseneath New Moon, was descended from the finest British lines of Wolvey, Waideshouse and Sollershot, both her parents having been imported.

Next a selective breeding program was embarked upon using Katherine Hayward's Huntingtonhouse strain; the Briarwoods belonging to Bettina King and Barbara Langdon; Ruth Birmingham's Lochcrest; Barbara Keenan's Elfinbrook Simon line; Michael Collinges' Purstons; and imports from Whitebriar.

Patricia Storey has always sought type and soundness in her dogs. She has never used a "fashionable" stud unless the feeling was strong that he would contribute to her Lonsdale lines.

Patricia notes, "Our dogs have given us much pleasure and we are extremely proud of them." Hardly a wonder when one considers that these dogs include an impressive 22 champions, all but six of them owner-handled!

MAC-KEN-CHAR

Mac-Ken-Char West Highland White Terriers was founded during the mid-1960s by Joanne Glodek and her daughter Jaimi Glodek at Severn, Maryland. In the beginning, breeding and showing was very limited, based on the early bloodlines of Champion Cruben Dextor and Champion Elfinbrook Simon.

In 1968, the Glodeks purchased a seven-year-old dog bred by Edward Danks. This was Champion Battison's Good Friday, and in two litters he sired six champions giving Joanne and Jaimi their foundation stud, Champion Mac-Ken-Char's Friday's Child.

Friday's Child altogether sired 17 champions, including the Glodeks' foundation dam, Mac-Ken-Char's Wild Irish. For the seven champions she gave Joanne and Jaimi, Wild Irish was the recipient of the West Highland-White Terrier Club of America's Brood Bitch award.

In 1970, Al Ayers imported a Westie for the Glodeks from England to introduce the Keithall line into their breeding program. This dog, Champion Keithall Pilot, became the first terrier to win Best in Show at the Puerto Rico Kennel Club in 1974. To make the event even more exciting, he was handled by the 12-year-old Jaimi Glodek.

Keithall Pilot and Wild Irish later produced the Top-Winning Breeder-Owner-Handled Westie of the time, known as Best in Show American and Bermudian Champion Mac-Ken-Char's Irish Navigator.

Am. and Ber. Ch. Mac-Ken-Char's Irish Navigator, by Ch. Keithall Pilot ex Mac-Ken-Char's Wild Irish, is taking Best of Breed at the Devon Dog Show, a victory he repeated the same weekend at Montgomery County 1984. This distinguished winner and sire is owned by Joanne and Jaimi Glodek, Severn, MD.

Irish Navigator began his career at nine months of age in Canada by winning Best Puppy in Show under author and judge Anna K. Nicholas, who saw his potential and encouraged the Glodeks to go on with showing this dog, predicting that he would go far, a prediction which turned out to be exactly accurate!

At age 17 months, in 1982, Navigator completed his American Championship at the Indiana Specialty under breeder-judge Dorothea Daniell-Jenkins. The following day he won Best of Breed over 13 "specials."

While earning his Bermuda title, Navigator took four Groups and a Best in Show. The following week he won his first American Group and Best in Show. That same year he won Best of Breed in the Specialty at Montgomery County over the largest Westie turnout in the history of this show, 192 Westies entered, judged by Mrs. Thelma Brown. Irish Navigator, known as "Gregory" at home and by friends, epitomizes what every breeder dreams of achieving. His record, which follows, says it all.

He has taken 12 Bests in Show and 14 Bests in Specialty; was named Number One Westie 1986 (all systems), Top Sire all breeds 1987, Top Terrier Sire 1987 and 1989, and also Top Westie Sire 1986, 1987, 1988 and 1989; has earned the distinction of Top-Producing Westie of All Time as well as Top-Winning Breeder-Owner-Handled Westie of All Time. Currently he has sired 85 champions (25 of them either owned or bred by Mac-Ken-Char), and in 1987, Gregory broke a record by siring 24 champions in one year. He is the sire of 34 specialty winners to date.

Mac-Ken-Char has either owned or bred 70 champions of which outstanding accomplishments include: 1984, Best of Breed at WHWTCA Montgomery County, Champion Mac-Ken-Char's Irish Navigator; 1985, Best of Breed at WHWTCA Roving Specialty, Champion

Ch. Mac-Ken-Char's White Shadow winning the Terrier Group at the States Kennel Club Dog Show at age 18 months. He went on to win Best in Show under judge Florise Hogan, and followed through with another Group the next day. Owned by Shane Albee and Mac-Ken-Char Kennels.

A "special" in 1989, **Ch. Mac-Ken-Char's White Shadow,** by Ch. Honeyhill's White Lightning ex Ch. Mac-Ken-Char's Scarlet O'Hara was bred by Ernest Stanley and owned by Mac-Ken-Char and Joan Stanley. This is a double grandson of the famed Irish Navigator, and is pictured taking Best of Winners at Ramapo.

Mac-Ken-Char's Onederboy; 1987, Best in Sweepstakes WHWTCA Roving Specialty, Champion Mac-Ken-Char's Major Motion; 1988, Best in Sweepstakes, WHWTCA Montgomery County, Champion BJ's Lady Mac-Ken-Char; 1984 and 1985, Best of Breed at Devon, Champion Mac-Ken-Char's Irish Navigator; Best of Breed at Hatboro, 1978, Champion D'Alexa's Mister Mac-Ken-Char; 1985 and 1987, Champion Mac-Ken-Char's Irish Navigator; 1981, Champion Woodbriar Watchman (W.D.); 1985, Champion Mac-Ken-Char's Ms. Mariner (W.B., B.O.W.); 1989, Champion Mac-Ken-Char's White Shadow (W.D., B.O.W.); 1987, Winners Bitch and Best of Winners at Hatboro, Champion Rodeb Scruples Mac-Ken-Char; Best in Sweepstakes at Great Lakes Terrier Association (gaining possession of the Perpetual Trophy with three wins), 1982, Champion Mac-Ken-Char's Irish Fantasy; 1984, Champion Mac-Ken-Char's Onederboy; and 1987, Champion Glengidge Moxie Mac; Best in Sweepstakes at West Highland White Terrier Club of Greater Baltimore (permanent possession of the Memorial Trophy with three wins), 1984, Champion Mac-Ken-Char's Irish Invader; 1985, Champion Mac-Ken-Char's Onederboy, and Champion BJ's Madam Mac-Ken-Char.

This very notable bitch was the first homebred champion produced at the Merryhart Kennels owned by Mr. and Mrs. J.W. Eberhardt, Encinitas, CA. **Am., Can. and Mex. Ch. Merryhart Pettipants** was sired by Ch. Elfinbrook Simon, Best in Show Westminster 1962, ex Ch. Kirk o'the Glen Merryhart. Pettipants was Best of Breed at the WHWTC 1967 Specialty. She was the dam of three champions.

MERRYHART

Merryhart West Highland Terriers, owned by Naomi and Jim Eberhardt of Encinitas, California, no longer is active as a kennel. However, the Eberhardts' accomplishments during their years of involvement in this field have been such as to make them among the foremost Westie people in the United States. The first homebred champion at Merryhart was American, Canadian and Mexican Champion Merryhart Pettipants who was a daughter of Champion Elfinbrook Simon out of the first Westie the Eberhardts owned, American, Canadian, and Mexican Champion Kirk O'the Glen Merryhart, the dam of four champions. Pettipants was a Group winner, and Best of Breed at the Specialty in California. She was the dam of three champions.

The first male belonging to the Eberhardts was American, Canadian, Mexican Champion Weaver's Drummond, a Best in Show winner whom they purchased from Ida Weaver when he was but eight weeks of age. Naomi showed him to all of his wins, which included the California Sweepstakes in 1967. Drummond sired 15 champions.

One of Drummond's outstanding sons was American, Canadian, Mexican Champion Merryhart Special Edition, who finished at eleven months of age, and went on to win

Am., Can. and Mex. Ch. Weaver's Drummond is a Best in Show winner and the sire of 15 champions. By Ch. Ugadale's Artists Model ex Ch. Weaver's Highland Jewel. Bred by Ida Weaver; owned by Mr. and Mrs. J.W. Eberhardt.

Best in Show under the ownership of Don Sell. Special Edition attended his first show, a Specialty, at age seven months, taking Winners Dog. His dam was Merryhart Pettipants.

American and Mexican Champion Merryhart Sound Off was a marvelous Drummond daughter, her dam having been Merryhart Promises Promises. Sound Off was Best of Breed at the National Roving Specialty in 1975, and was Best of Winners previously at the California Specialty. She was shown only eight times in the classes; four times as a "special." Her accomplishments include producing four champions, among them American and Mexican Champion Merryhart Love Child

Am. and Mex. Ch. Merryhart Honest John, by Ch. Finearte Dove's Beau ex Merryhart Plushbottom Belle, a Group Winner from the 1960s and the sire of 25 champions. Owned by Mr. and Mrs. J.W. Eberhardt.

(co-owned with Helen Love) and Champion Merryhart Cheerio.

Another outstanding Drummond daughter was American and Mexican Champion Merryhart Tattletale. She was a proud Terrier Group winner, Best of Opposite Sex at the California Specialty, and the dam of five champions, including American, Canadian, and Mexican Champion Paddy Whack and Champion Merryhart Buttermilk.

The Eberhardts imported Champion Finearte Dove's Beau, by English Champion Waideshouse Waterboy from English Champion Cedarfell Messenger Dove from

Am., Can. and Mex. Ch. Dreamland's Councillor was bred by A. and M. Kaye, Dreamland Kennels, Canada. Owned by Mr. and Mrs. J.W. Eberhardt, Councillor was sired by Ch. Dreamland's Cyclone ex Dreamland's Powder. A Group winner and the sire of 24 champions.

England. Beau sired for them four champions (out of Champion Merryhart Tattletale), one of which was Best of Winners and Best of Opposite Sex at the National Roving Specialty and Best in Sweepstakes in the National Roving Specialty in 1974. He was a multiple-Group winner, but best of all, he was the sire of 26 champions!

The fourth of Beau's champions was American, Canadian, and Mexican Champion Merryhart Paddy Whack, out of Champion Merryhart Tattletale. He was a Best in Show winner and a multiple Group-winning dog, plus the sire of four champions.

Winning Best in Show, **Am., Can. and Mex. Ch. Merryhart Paddy Whack,** by Ch. Finearte Dove's Beau ex Am. and Mex. Ch. Merryhart Tattletale. This exciting win took place at Ensenada, B.C. Owned by Mr. and Mrs. J.W. Eberhardt.

Beau's son, Honest John, in his turn sired two outstanding daughters from Champion Merryhart Sound Off from two different litters. The first, American and Mexican Champion Merryhart Love Child, was Best of Winners from the puppy class at the National Specialty with Montgomery County in 1975 at just ten months of age. She also continued to do considerable winning, handled at first by Naomi Eberhardt then later specialed by a professional handler. She was the dam of four champions from three litters.

in 1976; the brothers Champion Merryhart Jumpin' Jack, who was sold, and American and Mexican Champion Merryhart Honest John, who was kept—Jack and John were from Merryhart Plushbottom Belle. John was Best in Sweepstakes at

The second daughter was Champion Merryhart Cheerio, who gained her first points in the form of a four-point "major" at Hatboro from the puppy class at age ten months, also Best of Opposite Sex over "specials." Cheerio was Reserve Winners the next day from the puppy class at the 1976 National Specialty at Montgomery. In fact she took two Best in Sweepstakes, one of them at the National.

American and Mexican Champion Merryhart Adam Act Up, by Paddy Whack ex Cheerio, was a Sweepstakes and a multiple Group winner and the sire of three champions.

The Eberhardts purchased the lovely American, Canadian, and Mexican Champion Dreamland's Councillor from the Kayes in Canada when he was one year old, already a Canadian Champion, and had earned Top Westie Puppy in Canada. Naomi finished him to his title in the United States and Mexico. He became the sire of 14 champions. He was sired by Champion Dreamland's Cyclone ex Dreamland's Powder.

American, Canadian, and Mexican Champion Merryhart Aspen Able, by Champion Dreamland's Councillor ex Merryhart Bon Bon was a widely acclaimed dog, noted for his outstanding head. After some time, Able, along with Councillor, went to the Kayes for their Dreamland strain in Canada. Able sired 13 champions. Naomi and Jim Eberhardt showed their dogs themselves almost entirely unless otherwise stated. They have made up a total of 76 Westie champions. It is interesting to note that these tremendously successful breeders purchased their foundation bitch when starting out; and later, over a period of years, bought four males. The rest of the champions were their own homebreds. A record to be regarded with deep admiration.

ORION

Orion Westies at Dix Hills, New York, is owned by Ida and Joe Keushgenian who have been in the breed since the mid-1970s, during which time they have completed championship on 15 Westies of their own breeding.

Ch. Cynosure Orion the Hunter, by Ch. Illusion's Sir Gaylord Scott ex Ch. Har-Tis Cynosure Ursa Minor. Handled here by William Ferrara for owners Ida and Joe Keushgenian Dix Hills, NY.

Top dog at this kennel is without a doubt Champion Cynosure Orion the Hunter, who was their first West Highland and their first champion. He is the foundation of the entire Orion line.

This outstanding dog produced 14 champions in his lifetime including a Best in Show and specialty winner.

Ch. Cynosure Orion's Morning Star, by Ch. Cynosure Orion the Hunter ex Ramona O'Ragain. Owned by Orion Westies, Ida and Joe Keushgenian.

"Sport" himself was one of the Top Ten Westies for the years 1978 and 1979. His influence still is being strongly felt in this breed, his genes being in some of today's leading Westie winners.

Bred from an English background, Orion the Hunter goes back to Champion De Go Hubert and Whitebriar lines on his sire's side, and to Champion Elfinbrook Simon and Champion Monsieur Aus der Flerlage on his dam's. The American lines in his pedigree have as their source Flogan and Prosswick Kennels.

Orion the Hunter sired a daughter, Champion Cynosure Orion's Morning Star, who was handled by Ida to an impressive array of wins including winning a Terrier Group from the classes at her very first show—this momentous occasion was under judge Robert Moore. She earned Number Two Westie Bitch in the United States for 1980. Other particularly pleasing wins have included Best of Opposite Sex to Best of Breed at the parent club's Montgomery County Specialty; and Best of Breed at the Indiana Specialty, plus numerous Group placements, which always are fun, along the way. Morning Star's dam goes back into the well-known English kennel Famecheck.

Currently the Keushgenians are having fun with Champion Orion's Rising Sun, their beautiful Hunter son who has made his presence felt in the Westie ring. Orion's Rising Sun was born in 1988. This youngster's first win was at age seven months when he went Best of Opposite Sex in Sweepstakes at the Indiana Specialty. He completed his title by going Best of Winners in the regular classes and went Best in Sweepstakes at the West Highland White Terrier Club of Greater New York Specialty, and was campaigned as a "special." "Sunny" was a product of grandfather-to-granddaughter breeding. His dam was Champion Orion's Altair, whose pedigree traces back to Birkfell, Pillerton and Famecheck Kennels.

The Hunter himself died at age 12 years.

Ida is a former President of the West Highland White Terrier Club of Greater New York, an office she held for five years. Also for three years she served on the parent club board.

Now she has also been judging Sweepstakes classes, including Montgomery County, the National Specialty, with a record entry of 93. She also has judged Sweepstakes in Texas and California.

O'THE RIDGE

O'The Ridge Westies in Barrington, Illinois, is owned, very successfully, by Marjadele Schiele, who has been involved with these little dogs for, as she says, "longer than she cares to remember."

A tremendously important influence on her dogs of the past decade has been the noted Champion Pinmoney Puck, the winner of ten Bests in Show; Number One Terrier, Terrier Type System, 1974.

Puck sired an impressive 18 champions, including Marjadele Schiele's Champion Buddy O'The Ridge who himself has sired 11 champions.

Littermates Champion Barley and Higgins O'The Ridge both carry two lines to Puck, which have excelled in this splendid dog's type and quality.

Barley and Higgins, handled by their owner, took their earliest "majors" at age eight months. Barley

Ch. Pinmoney Puck taking Best in Show at Baltimore County in 1973. This dog co-owned by Barbara Keenan, who imported him, and Marjadele Schiele.

finished in a blaze of glory going Winners Bitch from the Bred-by Exhibitor Class at Montgomery County over a highly competitive turnout of 98 bitches; this on top of her five-point "major" at the South-

ern Texas Specialty with a Best of Winners and Best of Opposite Sex. Higgins also finished on this occasion with five points, and took Best in Sweepstakes there, too. Barley and Higgins were also both shown to Canadian championship.

During 1984, out as "specials," these two accounted for an aggregate total of 21 Bests of Breed, 20 Bests of Opposite Sex, and ten Group placements. Barley won the Terrier

Ch. Heritage Farm Jenny Jump Up, C.D., C.G., is pictured, with her handler Landis Hirstein, at Westminster 1970 winning Best of Breed under noted Westie expert Mrs. Barbara Keenan for owner, Marjadele Schiele, O'The Ridge Westies, Barrington, IL. The first American-bred Westie bitch in 27 years to win this award at the Garden, and also she is the first Westie bitch to win a Best in Show, which she has done on multiple occasions.

Group at Champaign, Illinois, and Group second at Jaxon, Michigan.

To add to the fun she had with them in regular-class competition, Marjadele has had some very exciting experiences with them as a Brace, entered in Brace Class competition. Their performance and evenness of type and quality make them a brace with which to reckon, as the competition has found out. They were Best Brace at the Canadian and Southeast Texas Specialties, plus twice at Montgomery County followed on one of these Montgomery occasions by Best Brace in Show. Additionally, they twice have been Best Brace in Show on an all-breed level.

Of course no one who has ever had the pleasure of seeing and judging that fantastic little bitch, Champion Heritage Farms Jenny Jump Up, ever could forget her. What a combination she made with her handler Landis Hirstein in hottest competition, as they carried away "honor after honor" all well deserved, for certainly Jenny Jump Up was a spectacular West Highland. Jenny achieved, during her show career, more honors than any Westie bitch preceding her had ever accomplished. These included four all-breed Bests in Show and three specialty Bests in Show. She was Top Westie under the Knight System and Number Four Terrier Bitch, Terrier Type System, for 1978—all of this prior to the time she had reached five-and-a-half years of age.

It is interesting to learn that Jenny had whelped 18 puppies prior to ever setting a paw into the ring!

Marjadele Schiele acquired Jenny, a daughter of Champion Monsieur Aus der Flerlage ex Champion Merryhart Sweet Pea, from the kennels belonging to Shirley Jean O'Neill. After finally getting her lead-broken and nicely groomed, Marjadele started showing. That was a bit of a trial, as at first Jenny clearly considered it great fun living up to her name—Jump Up—and gave her owner quite a workout. Once she learned what was expected of her, all ran smoothly, and from then on Jenny headed straight for the top. Her championship was gained in four weekends, and for frosting on the cake there were eight Breed wins and a Group second towards the end of 1977. Lanny Hirstein took her on the 1978 Florida circuit, which was smooth sailing all the way.

In addition to being one of the more beautiful Westies, Jenny had a personality to make everyone her own and her breed's friend. As the first American-bred Westie bitch to go Best in Show in 27 years, Jenny went a step further as she next became the first Westie of her sex to gain the Best in Show ribbon a second time.

Jenny's final title was a C.D. degree at ten years of age. At this same age, she also loved "going to ground" and working in the quarry.

Another noteworthy bitch of whom Mrs. Schiele speaks with affection is Champion Wishing Wells Water Baby, co-owned by her with Barbara Keenan. Water Baby finished her title under Bill Kendrick with some nice wins, but more notably over 60% of her offspring have become champions.

RIVERSIDE

Riverside West Highland White Terriers is proudly owned by Eve Varley, and located in Wichita, Kansas.

Eve's famed Champion Whitebriar Jollimont, "Monty" to friends, was born on April 20, 1981, a son of English Champion Jaimont of

Ch. Whitebriar Jollimont with handler Dora Lee Wilson placing second in Group at Peoria for owner Eve Varley, Riverside West Highland White Terriers, Wichita, KS.

Whitebriar (first in Group and Best of Breed at Crufts in 1983) from Whitebriar Jollity, a granddaughter of English Champion Whitebriar Jimmick. Monty's pedigree reads rather like a "Who's Who" of the Whitebriars with so many famous names behind him. It is easy to understand the success which Monty has met as a sire, and his valued influence both on Mrs. Varley's kennel and on the breed.

Ch. Riverside's Jolly Imp shows his type and quality plus beautiful balance. Dora Lee Wilson here is handling this notable dog for owner Eve Varley.

Among the champions sired by Monty is Eve's well-known Champion Riverside's Jolly Imp, from the lovely bitch Champion Whyte Imp's Nocturne, who is a daughter of Champion Carousel's Concert Master (Champion De Go Hubert ex Champion Impressario's Carousel) and Champion Jerojet's Encore (English, American and Canadian Champion Alpinegay Impression ex Champion Whitebriar Jouette). Jolly Imp is another to have made an exciting number of ring successes under Dora Lee Wilson's handling.

Monty's progeny gave a splendid account of themselves at the 1989 Montgomery show where six of his offspring and three grandkids were to be seen, including the stunning youngster Kilkerran Name of the Game, bred and owned by the Kompares, who was Reserve Winners Bitch.

ROUND TOWN

Round Town West Highland White Terriers is owned by Mr. and Mrs. R.D. Musser and located in Michigan at Laingsburg most of the year but during the summer on beautiful Mackinac Island.

Dan and Amelia Musser both have always loved and owned animals. Dan had a young guernsey heifer named "Spring Bouquet" in 4-H in Circleville, Ohio, and was given his first dog, a Smooth Fox Terrier, by his uncle George Hartman, as a very young boy.

Amelia was a teenager living in Upper Montclair, New Jersey, when her parents allowed her to acquire a sable and white Sheltie, named "Laddie," who in the course of events won a blue ribbon at Morris and Essex, which Amelia Musser says is "really why we are part of the fancy today." This is easily understandable when one stops to consider that George Hartman was one of the outstanding terrier men and A.K.C. directors whom the dog fancy has known and that Morris and Essex was an incomparable dog show.

Many years passed before the Mussers acquired their first dog, though they had intended to as newlyweds. At the International Kennel Club of Chicago, they saw their first Westie, and clearly it was "love at first sight." Ed Jenner happened by, and a friend who was with the Mussers knew him, so they asked Ed where they could acquire one of these little white darlings. "Why, B.G. Frame, of course" was the reply; and when Uncle George in Pennsylvania seconded that opinion, off went the Mussers to Indianapolis and Wigtown Kennels to visit Mrs. Frame. They did indeed own several Wigtown dogs, and good dogs they were; but they were not the Round Town foundation.

The foundation of Round Town was what Amelia describes as "a fluke of a puppy I was lucky enough to buy at the West Highland White Terrier Club of Northern Illinois Puppy Match." It took a bit of doing to persuade the breeder to part with her, but finally this was accomplished and she became Champion Rose Marie's Mean Mary Jean, finishing title for the Mussers at the Illinois Specialty under Dr. Booth. George Ward wanted to "special" her, but the Mussers had other commitments and decided to breed her instead.

Mary Jean might herself have been an "only pup," but she had a huge litter by an English import, Champion Warbonnet's Wolsey.

From this litter, CeCe and Cookie were finished, and CeCe (Champion Round Town Critics Choice) sent to Dorothea Daniell-Jenkins for breeding to Canadian Champion Rouge Manabu Zebedee. From this breeding came the Mussers' well-loved Dolly (Champion Wind Town All That Jazz), who was subsequently sent to Canada for breeding to a dog they had seen

Founder bitch at the Round Town Kennels, **Ch. Wind Town All That Jazz,** handled by George Ward to a good win under Westie breeder-judge and renowned Terrier authority, Mrs. Daniell-Jenkins. "Dolly," owned by Amelia and Dan Musser, completed title shortly thereafter.

and admired at Montgomery County, Champion Whitebriar Jeronimo.

This turned out to be a fantastic combination, producing the littermates Champion Round Town Ella J. Fitzgerald and Champion Round Town Duke J. Ellington.

The Mussers have imported, bought, and shown Westies from other breeders. But their best and principal line started from those three Champion Whitebriar Jeronimo–Champion Round Town All That Jazz breedings, of which

The outstanding bitch **Ch. Round Town Ella J. Fitzgerald** taking one of her Best in Show victories handled by George Ward for owners Amelia and Dan Musser. This win at Berrien K.C. in June 1986.

Champion Round Town Duke J. Ellington has sired 16 champions of record and three or more Best in Show and Specialty-winning get. The Mussers are now campaigning his son, Champion Snowbank Starr Shine, who is a multiple Best in Show and Specialty winner.

Champion Round Town Ella J. Fitzgerald is a top winning Westie bitch, with seven Bests in Show and several Specialty wins.

Amelia Musser says "The bitches have been beautiful movers, free whelpers, with lovely dispositions. From Whitebriar we locked in beautiful hard, white coats, lovely fronts and rears, and excellent tailsets."

There are several young bitches about to embark on show careers, and a half-dozen male puppies of exceptional promise, so the Mussers are optimistic as they contemplate the future.

RUDH'RE

Rudh'Re West Highland White Terriers is owned by Joan Graber in Middleton, Wisconsin, who was showing Collies in the late 1950s when she decided that she would enjoy having a smaller breed to share in the hobby. Her attention had been caught by Champion Elfinbrook Simon, and so she followed the sen-

A bit of Westie history from the 1950s, here is **Ch. Wishing Well's Wee Winklot** who gained her title at age two years. Here she is winning a Terrier Group under the most noted of all dog show judges, the late Alva Rosenberg. Owned by Joan Graber, this lovely bitch, very typical for this period, was bred by Barbara Worcester Keenan.

sible procedure of contacting Barbara Worcester regarding the possibility of purchasing a Simon daughter.

In making the inquiry, Joan had stated that she was looking for a brood bitch as a foundation for her kennel, knowing that she would probably end up showing it too. In 1962 Barbara sent Joan a seven-week-old daughter of Champion Snowcliff Patrician ex Champion Lawrenton Wee Maggie, the latter a Simon daughter. She became Champion Wishing Well's Wee Winklot gaining her title at about two years of age.

As fate would have it, Winkie never made it as a brood bitch, although she fared nicely in the show ring where her wins included several Group placements—among them a first under Alva Rosenberg. She was to be bred to Simon, but when the time came for that to happen it was found that she could not be bred naturally, which was a disappointment to all concerned. Barbara was kind enough, however, to send Joan another bitch, one which she had brought over from England, realizing that what Joan had really wanted was one on which to found her own line. This one came to Joan at age five months and eventually became Champion Whitebriar Jema. She was a combination of Whitebriar Famecheck and Fyezwfield bloodlines. So it was that Jema became Joan Graber's foundation bitch rather than Winkie who had originally been intended for this role in the kennel's history. Later on, Winkie was bred to Simon, successfully producing a nice litter.

Meanwhile Jema, having taken

Ch. Rudh'Re Fionn Sian who finished title in nine shows, always owner-handled and groomed by Joan Graber. She was the first big winner for Rudh' Re Westies.

necessarily divided between the two. Despite this shared attention, Judy really did all concerned proud with such victories as Best of Breed at the WHWTC of Northern Ohio (held in conjunction with Chagrin Valley) where she then went on to Best in the Terrier Group under judge Peter Knoop. In limited showing, from 1969 through 1972, Judy had eight Group placements of which five were firsts.

When bred to Champion Reanda Byline Pisces, Judy produced Champion Rudh'Re Glendenning; and when bred to Pisces's sire, Champion Monsieur Aus der Flerlage, she produced Champion Rudh'Re Cantie Peigi, who was Reserve Winners Bitch from the Puppy Class at the 1972 Montgomery County National Specialty.

Joan stopped showing Judy shortly after Glendenning finished as she of course could not herself

over as the foundation bitch, was bred to Champion Elfinbrook Simon, thus producing Champion Rudh'Re's Jillet, the only bitch in this litter. This youngster was sold to Allan and Marlene Kotlisky, Collie breeders who were interested in a Westie on a puppy-back arrangement. When Jillet was ready to be bred, Joan wanted to linebreed on Simon, so in 1967 Jillet was bred to Champion MacRowdy O'The Ridge, who not only was himself a Simon son but whose dam was Champion Wishing Well's Water Baby, a litter sister to Wee Winklot. From this breeding came Champion Rudh'Re Fionn Sian, known as Judy, who finished in nine shows, always owner-groomed and handled. During this period Joan was still showing the Collies so her attention was

Ch. Rudh'Re Glendenning, bred and owned by Joan Graber, Middleton, WI. By Ch. Reanda Byline Pisces ex Ch. Rudh' Re Fionn Sian.

take both of them into "specials." She had, however, enlisted the help of a friend to take one of them for her at the 1972 Montgomery, thus both were there, and she was pleased that Judy was one of the bitches pulled out for consideration.

was one of six males who made the cut under Mrs. Hartley in the breed ring.

At this point Joan Graber started to concentrate principally on her Westies rather than the Collies, although even then it was not her

Ch. Rudh'Re Glendenning bred and owned by Joan Graber.

With the breeding to Pisces which produced Glendenning, the Branston bloodlines were introduced to Rudh'Re's program. Champion Rudh'Re Glendenning, known as Dennis, completed title when age 14 months, after having won Best in Sweepstakes at the WHWTCA Roving Specialty under Thelma Adams. Three months later, Sylvia Kearsey awarded him Best in Sweepstakes at the annual national in conjunction with Montgomery County in 1972. It was also exciting that he

habit to show more than a dog and a bitch in the classes and Dennis in for "specials." When Dennis retired, the emphasis turned from campaigning a "special" to finishing at least one champion annually. With this, Dennis continued to do his part by turning out to be an excellent sire reproducing his good qualities in his offspring. By 1978 he had become the sire of many champions, most of which had gained the title owner-handled. Especially exciting was his first champion, who at age 13 months went from Winners Bitch to Best of Opposite Sex at the 1973 Montgomery show. This was Champion Briarpatch Raggamuffin, then co-owned by Joan. It was equally thrilling to watch her go Best of Breed from the Veterans' Class at the 1979 WHWTCA Specialty at Montgomery, handled by her owner.

Deciding that more "Simon" needed to be brought back into the line, Champion Rudh'Re Cantie Peigi was bred to Lead Hill's Patrick Henry, whose sire was a litter broth er to Mac-Rowdy. A bitch from that litter was subsequently bred to Dennis to produce Champion Rudh'Re Glenfinnan in 1977. "Finn" also was a splendid producer, but Joan was seeking a stud who would give the bone and elegance she admires. She tried several breedings which brought in other bloodlines, including Champion Greenbriar Gamblin' Man, who was a son of Champion Merryhart Happy Hobo out of a Champion Monsieur Aus der Flerlage granddaughter. A bitch from that cross was then bred to Glenfinnan to produce Rudh'Re Fennora.

Ch. Rudh'Re Roderick Dhu, by Ch. Waterford of Wyndam, is one of the splendid Westies owned by Joan Graber.

Joan Graber also co-owned a Glendenning granddaughter, Champion Byline Kilt O'Wicken, by Champion Pillerton Pride ex Champion Byline Highland Quince, whom she bred to Glenfinnan. From this came a typy bitch who remained relatively small, Rudh'Re Twalpennies.

Having seen Champion Whitebriar Jeronimo shortly after the Frasers had acquired him, Joan was eager to have what she considered a proper bitch to outcross to him, to maintain the elegance she likes and add a bit more bone. The Glenfinnan daughter, Rudh'Re Fennora, was selected, and Joan got everything for which she had hoped in the dog who became Champion Rudh'Re The MacNeil and a bitch, who although never finished has produced two champions sired by two different males.

In 1988 Joan Graber outcrossed a daughter of The MacNeil from Rudh'Re Twalpennies to Champion Waterford of Wyndam. The small dog she kept from this finished to become Champion Rudh'Re Roderick Dhu; and there is a bitch who will also be shown.

SHELLY BAY

Shelly Bay West Highland White Terriers is owned by Marilyn S. Foster at Simsbury, Connecticut. Although interested in the breed since the late 1970s, Marilyn did not really start on the Westie road to success until December 1985 with the acquisition of her Shelly Bay foundation bitch. This was Holyrood's Ms. Mayhem, known as Shelby, co-owned with Judith Francisco of Holyrood Kennels.

Shelby completed her championship in stiff New England competition, taking Best of Breed from the classes after gaining her final four-point "major" under the respected authority Mrs. W. Potter Wear.

It is as a producer, however, that Shelby has won widest fame and admiration, very justly as I am certain our readers will agree. Glenfinnan's Something Dandy was the sire selected for Shelby's first litter. To say that it was successful is an understatement!

From these puppies came future Champion Holyrood's Hootman O'Shelly Bay, who grew up to become a famous name in Westies as Top Winning West Highland White Terrier for 1989 and 1990, gained by his All-Breed Bests in Show, his Terrier Group victories, and his specialty show Bests of Breed.

Manley, as he was known,

made his first Montgomery County Kennel Club appearance in 1988 when he gained the Best of Winners honor. In 1989 and 1990, he returned, each time going to the top of his breed. Manley was sold, at age seven months, to Dr. James and Elizabeth Boso under whose ownership and the handling of Mark George he has become a living legend.

Manley's three littermates also have proven themselves to be Westies of exceptional merit. Champion Holyrood Hootnanny O'Shelly

At only eight months old, here is the future big-time winner who became **Ch. Holyrood's Hootman O'Shelly Bay** with his handler Mark George winning at the Seattle Roving Specialty soon after his purchase by the Bosos. This is a handsome depiction of balance, proportion, and a correct silhouette for the breed. Owned by Dr. and Mrs. Boso.

Bay, known as Fanny, started out at age three and a half months by winning Best Puppy in an important terrier match under noted professional handler Bob Clyde, gained top honors at several other matches, then at age six and a half months was Reserve Winners Bitch from the Puppy Class at Montgomery County 1988, following this by winning the Sweepstakes at the San Francisco Specialty in 1989. Fanny took time off for a litter after this, but then set out to complete her championship with Bergit Cody.

The other male from this litter, Champion Holyrood's Hopscot O'Shelly Bay, known as Barnaby, was Reserve Winners Dog at the William Penn WHWTC Specialty in 1989 under judge Ed Dixon and completed his title with a four-point "major" under Michele Billings.

Lastly, the other bitch, Holyrood's Ha'Penny O'Shelly Bay, is pointed and completing her title with handler Jay Richardson.

One of the most exciting dog show occasions for Shelly Bay we are certain was when Shelby won the Brood Bitch Class with her son and daughter, Hootman and Hootnanny.

As co-owner of Champion Holyrood's Liza with a "Z," Number Three among Westie bitches in 1987, Shelly Bay co-bred a litter in March 1989 that included three very special puppies: Holyrood's Miss High Falutin, who was Sweepstakes winner at the WHWTC of Indiana Specialty 1990; Holyrood's Karly With A "K," Best of Winners and Best in Sweepstakes at the recent 1990 WHWTC of Washington, D.C. Specialty Show; and Holyrood's Here Comes The Son, "Gibby," owned by Shelly Bay, who is pointed and being presented sparingly by Jay Richardson.

Here Comes The Son and Shelby produced two outstanding offspring born in January 1990. They are Holyrood's Wild Bill of Shelly Bay, who was Best of Opposite Sex at the

Fabulous Westie puppies, these are, *left to right*, **Penny, Black, Ready, Fanny** and **Manley,** at home at Shelly Bay. Marilyn Foster, owner, Simsbury, CT. A notable display of tremendous quality in young members of the breed.

The wonderful bitch behind the noted winners at Shelly Bay. This is Shelby, **Ch. Holyrood's Ms. Mayhem,** a daughter of Ch. Kilkerran's The Joker is Wild ex Ch. Whitemount Frolic TWA. Owned by Marilyn S. Foster, she is the dam of Ch. Holyrood's Hootman O'Shelly Bay who won Best of Breed at Montgomery in 1989 and 1990 among other show triumphs.

WHWTC of Greater New York at age eight months in September 1990; and Holyrood's Hotspur of Shelly Bay, who is particularly promising and for whom his owner has high hopes that he may carry on in the Manley tradition. Such accomplish-ments as Shelly Bay has attained over so short a period of time are truly notable, and speak louder than mere words ever could of the superb quality of Shelby and other splen-did Westie dogs and bitches who have brought all this about.

SILVERY DEE

Silvery Dee West Highland White Terriers, at Washington Crossing, Pennsylvania, is owned by Martha W. Black, who has been active in Westies since 1968 when she purchased several dogs from the American kennel known as Tyndrum, owned by Mrs. Anthony M. Walters.

All breeding and showing at Silvery Dee was built on the Tyndrum lines until 1985 when Champion

Best of Breed at the WHWTC of Greater NY 1987, **Am. and Can. Ch. Jack The Lad of Jopeta from Purston,** son of Ch. Jopeta Jamie Mac Phert ex Darolam Barbarella Gelba. Mrs. Martha Black, owner ; George Wright, handler.

Jack The Lad of Jopeta from Purston was imported from England. This dog was extensively shown for Mrs. Black by George Wright, and was Number One Westie for 1987 in the United States.

A Scottish import, Champion Pilot of Keithall, was first shown as a "special" at the WHWTCA at Mont-gomery County during 1987, where he took Best of Breed, handled by Enid Wright.

Pilot was campaigned throughout 1988 and 1989. During these two years he won Best of Breed at the Westminster Kennel Club along with important Terrier Groups and an All-Breed Best in Show. Bred by Mrs. C. K. Bonas, Pilot is a son of Champion Exultation of Tasman ex Arnholme April Shower.

SKAKET

It was in 1966 that Nancy Gauthier of North Andover, Massachusetts, bought her first Westie, which was also her first dog. She needed a small dog owing to family circumstances at that time, and as it happened the only purebreds of which she was aware (she referred to them then as "thoroughbreds") were Collies, German Shepherds and Poodles. That long ago she had not the slightest idea how many different breeds and types of dog actually were available.

She decided that the sensible procedure would be to visit a pet shop, but on first look she saw little that she considered appealing. Noting her lack of enthusiasm, the owner of the shop took her upstairs where the older puppies were kept. And there was "Terrie." She was a three-month-old Westie scratching at the crate, wagging her tail, and looking at Nancy with that wonderful Westie expression so dear to the hearts of all who know the breed. It was instant love on both sides.

A friend told Nancy about an obedience class which sounded like fun. So off she and Terrie went. At that point Nancy never had seen an adult Westie. The obedience instructor suggested she pay a visit to Shirley and Fred Nicholas, and it was Shirley who started Nancy out in the world of breeding and showing dogs. Much to the surprise of Shirley, and Nancy, who was totally "green" on such subjects, it turned out that Terrie not only was herself a good-quality Westie but her pedigree carried the lines of some extremely prominent Westie strains. Based on this, Terrie, it was decided, should have a litter. This led to her becoming the foundation behind the famed and widely admired Skaket Westies.

Am. and Can. Ch. Pilot of Keithall, by Ch. Exultation of Tasman ex Arnholme April Shower, winning Best of Breed at the WHWTCA Specialty in conjunction with Montgomery County in 1987. Handled by Enid Wright for owner, Mrs. Martha W. Black.

In 1970, Nancy acquired Pookie II from Shirley Nicholas. Bred to Champion Lochness MacTavish, C.D., Pookie produced Champion Skaket's Chunkies, U.D. It is the combination of these two lines that produced International, Bermudian, Mexican, Canadian and American Champion Skaket's Candy Man, C.D.X., T.D., C.G., T.T.

Nancy Gauthier retired in 1983 from breeding Westies though she does allow her dogs to be used at stud when folks have bitches they wish to breed to them. Her daughter, Mitzi, who shared the interest and hobby with her mother from the beginning, decided to carry on with Skaket breeding. Mitzi is at the helm and doing very successfully as both a breeder and as an exhibitor.

Handling her Champion Skaket's Taffy, C.D. to Winners Bitch at Montgomery County and her Champion Skaket's Katie, C.D. to a Terrier Group from the classes are just

Beating three champions his first time in the ring, the future **FCI Int., Mex., Ber., Can., and Am. Ch. Skaket Candy Man, C.D.X., T.D., C.G., T.T.** at age 13 months. Bred and owned by Nancy Gauthier and Mitzi Gauthier, Skaket Westies, N. Andover, MA.

a couple of examples of how well she is doing; plus the breeding and handling of Champion Skaket's Maximillian has been an exciting experience.

Skaket Westies average only about one litter a year, as the Gauthiers concentrate on producing *quality* rather than quantity, and having the dogs as a source of fun.

Candy Man would undoubtedly be considered Skaket's "star," with his impressive array of titles and his prestigious individual successes. He is a Best in Show winner; has 17 times been Best Terrier

Ch. Whitebriar Jervish, by Whitebriar Jonfair ex Whitebriar Jossigny, was bred by Mrs. J.E. Beer. Owners, Jodine Vertuno and Mary E. Finley, Naperville, IL.

plus numerous other Group placements, the latter including Group Fourth at Montgomery County in 1981 and Group Second there in 1988, the latter from the Veterans' Class at age nine years; multiple Canadian Best in Show honors and first runner-up to Best in Show; at the 1983 Canadian "Show of Shows"; a Bermuda Best in Show; Stud Dog award from the WHWTCA; a Versatility award from the WHWTCA; and, at the start of his career, age 13 months, he topped three champions his first time in the ring to take Best of Opposite Sex. As a sire, Candy Man has 17

champions to his credit.

The Gauthiers, especially Nancy who started out in the obedience field, do not neglect obedience training and competition for their dogs, as you will note from the degrees listed after their names. Chunkies, for example, who is Candy Man's grandsire, was the first Westie to have received the Versatility award from the WHWTCA, and was a U.D.

SNO-BILT

Sno-Bilt Kennels, at Naperville, Illinois, originated as the home of some excellent Samoyeds owned by John and Jodine Vertuno, who started out with their dogs in obedience, where they earned C.D. and C.D.X. degrees, then into conformation where they gained championship honors. As Samoyed breeders, they felt that the dogs they were raising were built for snow, hence the kennel identification, Sno-Bilt.

The Vertunos raised and showed their Sammies for awhile and successfully, enjoying the breed. But while this was taking place they themselves added two family members, adorable little girls, who were being subjected to quantities of Sammy fur. So the decision was made that a smaller, less hairy breed should be selected, at least on a trial basis. It did not take John and Jodine long to select the West Highland White Terrier following a bit of study, research, and observation of the breed. The first of their Westies was purchased in the mid-1960s, and the first litter born a couple of years later. Jodine was not quite happy with the puppies, thus all were sold. Their next try as Westie breeders turned out to be far more successful, getting their activities under way. Champion Firrle D. Dee sired a very nice litter from Champion Sno-Bilt's Lobil's Abby. From this combination came Champion Sno-Bilt's Raggedee Ann, who was the Vertunos' first homebred Westie champion.

Dreamland's Mighty Patrol was purchased from Canada for breeding purposes, thus Sno-Bilt Westies were on their way. Raggedee Ann was bred producing Champion Sno-Bilt's Aquarius who was owner-handled to his title and who also won the Great Lakes Terrier Association Specialty in Illinois. The latter excit-

ing win from the Veteran's Class when seven years old under distinguished judge Dr. Josephine Duebler in 1977. Three years later, at ten years of age, he led the Veterans at Montgomery County.

Mrs. Vertuno decided that the importation of a top-quality dog from Mrs. J. E. Beer in England would benefit her breeding. And so, with Betsey Finley of Woodlawn Kennels as co-owner, she brought to America the dog Whitebriar Jervish, a decision which worked out well.

Jervish lived with Betsey Finley until both owners agreed that he was ready to start his show career in the United States, upon which he was turned over for campaigning to professional handler Bergit Cody. His title was gained with ease. Jervish also well lived up to Mrs. Vertuno's hopes in bringing him here when he became a West Highland Club of America Top Producer.

The Westie in whom Mrs. Vertuno takes particular pride is Best in Show Champion Sno-Bilt's Puzzle. Although not herself the breeder of this outstanding Westie, he is from her stock, his sire being out of a Sno-Bilt bitch and

The noted Terrier Group and Best in Show winner **Am. and Bah. Ch. Sno-Bilt's Puzzle** taking Best Terrier at Terre Haute April 1982. Jodine Vertuno owner; Carol Casurella, breeder.

A rear view of an excellent Westie in the show ring. **Ch. Kilkerran's 'N Wicket A Kut Above,** the famous "Kutter" is ready for the judge's inspection. Co-owner Nancy Spelke, handling.

sired by the stud dog she had suggested for that breeding to Carol Casurella.

Puzzle was handled throughout his entire show career by Jodine Vertuno, including during his tour of the Bahamas finishing his championship there and going on to Group second. His Best in Show wins were under judges Bob Wills, Anne Rogers Clark, and Alvin Tiedeman, respectively. Needless to say, Mrs. Vertuno found it extremely thrilling to accomplish all this with her owner-handled dog!

At the Great Lakes Specialty in 1983, Puzzle was Best of Breed, his young daughter adding special pride to the event by taking Winners Bitch, Best of Winners, and Best of Opposite Sex. Now retired, Puzzle has sired more than 50 champions for Sno-Bilt.

NANCY SPELKE

Nancy Spelke of Pasadena, California acquired her first Westie during the mid-1980s, Champion Kilkerran Matinee Idol, whom she herself showed through to the title. Sired by Champion Kilkerran The Joker is Wild ex Champion Kilkerran Moonstone, Matinee Idol was bred by Kathy and Wayne Kompare.

Next Nancy wanted another Westie to really campaign, which is how she became co-owner, handler and conditioner of Champion Kilkerran 'N Wicket A Kut Above, known to his friends as "Kutter"; Nancy co-owns him with Laura Moreno and his co-breeder, Kathleen Kompare.

Kutter began his show career in the classes in October 1987, finishing in nine shows with four "majors." In 1988 he started as a "special," and was campaigned for two exciting years by Nancy, retiring at the Westminster Kennel Club event of 1990.

Upon his retirement, Kutter had attained multiple All-Breed and Specialty Bests in Show; Best of Breed 138 times; had 100 Group placements including Best Terrier on 37 occasions.

Kutter was bred by Vicki Beets and Kathleen Kompare. Sired by Haweswalton Man About Town ex Champion Kilkerran Lady Guinevere, this American-bred Westie was born on October 1, 1984.

SWEET SOUND

Sweet Sound West Highland White Terriers is among the more recent additions to the ranks of top winning kennels in the breed, owned by Robert and Susan Ernst of Weston, Connecticut.

Ch. Principal's MacGyver, by Ch. Holyrood's Hot Shot ex Elsinore Plupurrfect O'Malley, was bred by Karen Polizzo, is handled by Kathleen Ferris, and is owned by Robert and Susan B. Ernst, Sweet Sound Kennels, Weston, CT. Pictured here winning his first Best in Show at Merrimack Valley K.C. under judge William Garvey.

The Ernsts entered the Westie fancy and dog-show world with the handsome young Champion Principal's MacGyver, known to his friends as "Mackie." He started his career winning Group Second and Group First as he completed his championship, then went on to become a Best in Show dog, a multi-Group winner and placer, and, in 1988, winner of the Kal Kan Award of Distinction, defeating a total of 760 Westies that year which made him Number One in breed systems and Number Five overall among show West Highland White Terriers in the United States. His Bests of

81

Breed add up to more than 100, including Specialty Shows. MacGyver's parents are Champion Holyrood's Hot Shot and Elsinore Plupurrfect O'Malley.

Recently joining the Westies at Sweet Sound, a new contender, Champion Biljonblue's Best of Times, "Timer" has made his presence felt having started out by taking Winners Dog at the William Penn Specialty and having remained undefeated in limited showing with eight Bests of Breed and two Group placements, all at less than 18 months age. He seems destined to follow in Mackie's paw prints. Timer was sired by Champion Biljonblue's Bee Gee; his dam Biljonblue's Miss Emily. Both Mackie and Timer are handled by Kathleen Ferris.

Ch. Skaket's Chunkies, U.D., C.G. is the grandsire of Ch. Skaket's Candy Man. Owned by Nancy and Mitzi Gauthier.

WEE MACK

Wee Mack Kennels, located in Java, New York, is owned by Mrs. Eileen McNulty, long a successful owner and fancier.

Among Mrs. McNulty's highly successful winners and producers one finds a most beautiful Australian import, American and Australian Champion MacPrain Machoman, a son of the noted Australian and New Zealand Champion Wistmill Woodpecker of Whitebriar ex Whitebriar Jillaroo, bred by

Mrs. Donahue, the well-known Australian breeder.

Mrs. McNulty really likes the Whitebriar bloodline, and has incorporated it considerably into her own strain. Another highly valued dog of hers is American and Canadian Champion Whitebriar Jesp, by Whitebriar Jimmick ex Jollity of

Right: At the Show of Shows in Canada, **Ch. Skaket's Candy Man** taking first runner up to Best in Show. Barbara Partridge handling for breeders-owners Nancy and Mitzi Gauthier.

Below: Taking Winners at Montgomery County in 1986, **Am. and Ber. Ch. Skaket's Taffy, C.D., C.G.,** is a Candy Man son from Briarton Bonnie Girl, bred and owned by Wayne B. Lindgren.

Whitebriar. This Group-winning dog is straight from the British Whitebriars, bred by Mrs. Beer and Miss Murphy.

Champion Wee Mack Heavy on the Mister, by Champion Whitebriar Jacksprat ex Champion Wee Mack Nitty Gritty, has done very well at the shows, handled to titular honors by Eileen's daughter, Susan McNulty.

WISHING WELL

Wishing Well Kennels have belonged to Barbara Keenan of Killingworth, Connecticut, since the late 1940s, and Barbara remains active and as enthused as she was at the very start. In the beginning, Mrs. Florence Worcester, Barbara's mother, and she were partners with the dogs. More recently, the dog-loving family members are in their third generation, with Barbara's daughter, Patty, showing all the enthusiasm and expertise for her own dogs as did Barbara herself. Patty breeds Beagles, so primarily Wishing Well is concerned with that breed; but there are still some marvelous West Highland Terriers belonging to Barbara. The galaxy of Westie stars who have been owned, bred or imported and campaigned at Wishing Well would fill a volume of their own. One after another they have come, Westies of superb quality who have reached their full potential for Wishing Well and for all Westies in the United States.

Barbara's first Westie champion was Champion Edgerstoune Candy, purchased from Mrs. Winant when Barbara was just 13 years old. Mrs.

Ch. Biljonblue's Best of Times taking a Group placement in March 1990. This young dog started his show career with a five-point "major" at the William Penn Specialty and was undefeated in limited showing with eight Bests of Breed and two Group placements at age 18 months. Owned by Robert and Susan Ernst, Sweet Sound Kennels, "Timer" is by Ch. Biljonblue's Bee Gee ex Biljonblue's Miss Emily and was bred by Biljonblue Kennels. Kathleen Ferris handler. Timer was Number Two Westie in U.S.A. for 1992.

Winant was a leading Westie breeder of her day.

In 1954 the renowned Champion Cruben Dexter came from England to Wishing Well; a dog of outstanding value as a sire and in the show ring. Dexter played a vital role in the foundation of several now leading bloodlines. Many were his admirers and Dexter gained championship with ease, becoming a Best in Show winner along the way.

Other famous Wishing Well Westies were English Champion Tulyar of Trenton and

Am. and Can. Ch. Whitebriar Jesp, by Whitebriar Jimmick ex Jollity of Whitebriar, was born in 1978 and was imported by Mrs. E. McNulty from English breeder Mrs. J.E. Beer and Miss M. Murphy. Pictured winning the Terrier Group at Conewango Valley in 1981.

Champion Symmetra Snip, both of whom lost little time in becoming American and Canadian Champions and Best in Show winners. They were high on the lists of outstanding show Westies, and it was Symmetra Snip who brought home the first Montgomery Best in Show trophy, most coveted of all awards for a Terrier—a stunning achievement. Champion Cruben Flash was still another notable member of the Wishing Well crew.

Then Champion Elfinbrook Simon arrived to join the Wishing Wells. This wonderful little dog had been less than a sensation in his native land, as sometimes happens with the "greats." But how that situation did change once Simon became "settled in" in the United States.

Unsuccessful in his first shows abroad, Simon who had been bred by the British breeders Mr. and Mrs. Mitchell, was sold by them, then purchased as a puppy from Len Pearson in England by the Worcesters. Feeling that all he needed was the time in which to mature, Barbara decided to try Simon out in Canada. A wise decision as he finished title there with three all-breed Bests in Show and a specialty Best. What more could anyone ask of a little dog just new to the country?

Then at three shows in the U.S., Simon got off to a flying start with a Group Third, then Best of Breed at the National Specialty. After a couple months, Barbara decided she would enjoy personally finishing him,

Ch. **Lymehills Birkfell Solstice** among the Best in Show winners from Wishing Well Kennels, handled here by Henry J. Sayres.

Simon's big year was to be 1962, which he started in Florida on that competitive circuit in George's charge. There he took several Bests in Show. For Westminster only Simon had been entered for handling by George. In fact, Barbara has been quoted as saying that George really was not anxious to show in New York anyway. He did finally allow himself to be persuaded to take Simon there, a decision helped along, we suspect, by Barbara's threat that unless George would do so, Barbara would show Simon herself.

Of course, the outcome provided the Westie fancy with one of its most momentous occasions. Champion Elfinbrook Simon found winning the Breed easy; the Terrier Group more of the same; and then there he was

Ch. **Pinmoney Puck** was a notable winner of the early 1970s for Barbara Keenan's Wishing Well Kennels.

which she did at the Indiana Specialty. She also gained two more Groups with him in Tennessee. By then she had decided that Simon was ready to go visit George Ward for his expert opinion and to discuss Simon's future. Although George already had two other Wishing Well dogs in his kennel at that time, he agreed to take on Simon if Barbara so wished. That year, at only three years of age, Simon placed Third in the Westminster Terrier Group.

in the vast ring for Best in Show. Simon looked around, obviously decided "I can do this" and he *did.* Best in Show at Westminster—the second such victory ever for a Westie there. What a thrilling experience! One's pleasure in a win cannot help being in accordance with the quality of the judging; and it would be impossible to find three more knowledgeable and stalwart Terrier men than John Marvin, himself a Westie breeder, making the breed selection; in the Group the esteemed owner of the Foxden Smooth Fox Terriers, James A. Farrell; and the noted Scottie breeder Heywood Hartley for the top award of Best in Show. These wins under so distinguished a panel would be delightful *anywhere;* but, at Westminster, the supreme American dog show, it must have been fantastic.

Only a single Westie previous to that time had won a Westminster Best in Show, 20 years earlier in 1942. On that occasion, it had been Mrs. Winant's lovely bitch, Champion Wolvey Pattern, whom she had imported from England for her Edgerstoune Kennels in New Hampshire. Simon and Pattern still stand on the record, one dog and one

bitch, as the only two Westminster Best in Show Westies to date.

The year having started off in so

Ch. Elfinbrook Simon winning his final Best in Show, at Harbor Cities K.C. in 1962, owner-handled by Mrs. Barbara Keenan. Simon retired soon after with 27 Best in Show awards to his credit including Westminster, of course.

spectacular a manner, it was decided that Simon would continue his career a while longer into the following month in 1962. During just two months following his Westminster victory, Simon won wherever he was entered through to Chicago International where he went Group Two. It was then settled that he would stay out until May, when Barbara decided definitely to take

Sw. and Am. Ch. Glenncheck May Be is owned by Pat Darby and Barbara Keenan, for whom William McFaddan is the handler. May Be is a specialty and an all-breed Best in Show winner.

him home, giving him a whirl as sort of a grand finale. Handled by Barbara, he made four shows, and Simon wound up Best Terrier at Springfield, Trenton, Harbor Cities and in Colorado, plus Bests in Show at the final two. One final appearance after that took him to the California Specialty which he won under judge Derek Rayne.

Simon's victories stand at 27 times Best in Show, plus many specialty shows and an imposing number of Terrier Groups. He also has important credits as a sire, his influence remaining today in the pedigrees behind important and influential descendents.

WIT'S END

Wit's End West Highland White Terriers, at Malone, New York is owned by Mrs. Joan Zwicker who has had Westies since the 1950s. Her first was a grandson of Champion Rowmore Ardifuer, which is where this love affair began.

Mrs. Zwicker's first litter produced Canadian Champion Zwicker's Bonnie Taps, sired by "Mrs. D.J.'s" Champion Shipmates Hannibal from Mrs. Zwicker's daughter of Glengorden Julie, whose sire was Champion Sollershot Sun Up. Julie had been sent to Canada as a stud fee "pick" puppy then back by May Pacey to Nora Kinnimonth. The sire was Rob Roy, an Alpin of Kendram son. Julie and Robbie eventually came into Mrs. Zwicker's hands to live out their days with her family.

Taps was shown at Westminster and was Winners Bitch under John Murphy. But as a widow with two young children, Joan Zwicker was unable to show Taps as much as she would have enjoyed doing, although she did finish her in Canada. Honors of particular merit won by Taps included the Bred-by Exhibitor award given by the Canadian West Highland Terrier Club in 1970; and the Bred-by Exhibitor Bitch award given by the West Highland White Terrier Club of America that same year.

Can. Ch. Zwicker's Bonnie Taps is from the first Westie litter produced at Wit's End Kennels in the 1960s. Winners Bitch at Westminster under judge John P. Murphy. Mrs. Joan Zwicker, owner, Malone, NY.

Another of Joan Zwicker's successful bitches was Hilltops Picadilly, one which was liked by Percy Roberts and Mrs. B. G. Frame during her show career. Cliff Hallmark finished this one for her owner from the American-bred Bitch Class, with her also winning two American-bred Bitch special awards, these in 1973 and 1974 from the West Highland White Terrier Club of America. Picadilly gained her Canadian title with the final points under Mrs. Doris Wear.

Boy Noel of Hilltop was also owned and shown by Joan Zwicker and he earned a special award from the West Highland White Terrier Club of America.

Since responsibilities at home are her first priority, Joan Zwicker does not travel far for dog shows; and since she lives in an area where shows are not numerous (or weren't until recently), her showing opportunities have been a lot less frequent than she would prefer.

The two Zwicker daughters, Penny and Candy, are also fond of the Westies, and, as young junior handlers, showed the dogs upon occasion. Joan Zwicker's interest continues, and now perhaps we will see her more frequently in the ring.

Am. and Can. Ch. Hilltop's Picadilly completing her Canadian title owner-handled by Mrs. Joan Zwicker, Wit's End Westies.

Westies in Canada

The first West Highland White Terrier to have been registered with the Canadian Kennel Club was a bitch named Calehaig who had been imported and was owned by Hugh Cameron from Toronto. She came to Canada from Scotland where she had been bred by S. MacLeod, and McLaren of Victoria, B.C. Mrs. Allan Blackburn of Salt Spring Island, British Columbia, was Alastair's breeder.

Westies have been known in Canada since the beginning of this century, and history tells us that they have been shown continuously

Left to right are **Rouge Tammymatt Madrigal** at age 13 months by Am. Ch. Wigtown Matthew ex Can. Ch. Tamoshanter's Lady Gordon; **Can. and Ber. Ch. Rouge Macabee Zebedee,** by Can. Ch. Jokar's Macabee ex Wigtown Mandy; and **Can. Ch. Cromarty Noelle of the Rouge,** by Am. Ch. Pillerton Prosper ex Can. Ch. Cromarty Annie Lauries. Zeb is a popular Canadian and U.S. stud, with seven Canadian champions and an American champion to his credit, the latter being the dam of the littermates Ch. Round Town Ella Fitzgerald and Ch. Round Town Duke J. Ellington. Madrigal and Zeb were bred by Mrs. Daniell -Jenkins; Noelle was bred by Mr. and Mrs. Lorne Gignac. All three are owned by Mrs. Daniell-Jenkins, Kennels of the Rouge, Pickering, Ontario, Canada. Photo courtesy of R.W.D. Photographics, Plattsville, Ontario.

in 1909 she was assigned #10862 by the C.K.C.

The first Canadian-bred West Highland registered was born in 1909, named Alastair, and added the title of Champion to this name when exhibited by owner D. B. since that time, being seen in competition there from coast to coast over the years.

Champion Alastair was followed to the title by Ardoch Model, Lothian Snowball, and Morag Bhan prior to 1916. Champion Rowmore Ardifuir belonging to Victor Blochin was the first Group-winning Westie in Canada; while the first Best in Show for the breed was Champion Edgerstoune Star Dust, owned by Misses Billings and Humby.

The Canadian West Highland White Terrier Club was founded in 1952 by an all-Canadian task force that included Mr. and Mrs. T. S. Adams, Victor Blochin, Mr. and Mrs. J. H. Daniell-Jenkins, Miss Edith Humby, Mr. and Mrs. Albert Kaye, Miss Nora Kininmonth, Mrs. H. C. Lefroy, Mr. and Mrs. J. N. Malcolm and Don Seabrook.

Also involved were two associate members from the United States, Mrs. S. H. Blue and Mrs. B. G. Frame.

Bencruachan Kennels, belonging to Victor Blochin, was one of tremendous early influence in Cana-

dian breeding of Westies from the 1930s until well into the 1950s. Their first to finish was in 1933, Champion Bencruachan Aetna, followed by Champion Bencruachan Cotopaxi in 1934, Champion Bencruachan Wendy in 1935 (one of only two gaining a title in the breed that year), D'Artagnon in 1938, Bambino in 1939, Aimee in 1940, Crystal in 1940 (another year in which only two Westies were finished in Canada), Jacqueline and Ray in 1949, and four individuals in 1950, Ardy, Bonnie, Punch and Tinker. Mistletoe and Snowflake added Champion to their names in 1951; Punch did so in 1952; Judy and Rita in 1953; Sporran and Squire in 1954; then, no other from this kennel until Champion Bencruachan White Heather did so in 1958.

Bencruachan Westies provided part of the foundation for Kennels of the Rouge and are to be found in the background of many other winning Westies.

Mr. Blochin passed away in the late 1970s, a man who contributed enormously to the progress and future of his much-loved breed in Canada. One of his most notable winners although not bearing the Bencruachan identification, was Champion Rowmore Ardifuir, the first Westie Group winner in Canada, and Grand Champion of Canada in 1937.

Other prominent early breeders, who were also founding members of the Canadian West Highland White Terrier Club,

Ch. Carroll's Haggis Basher, the first homebred Best in Show winner from Linda Carroll's Westies, Atlanta, GA. Handled by Dennis Kniola.

include Miss Edith Humby ("Highland", later known as "Humby's") and Mr. and Mrs. A. A. Kaye. We have already noted that the first Westie to win Best in Show in Canada belonged to Miss Humby, this one in co-ownership with Miss Rosamond Billings. More recently she has had a Best in Show winner in Champion Highland Arcturus.

Mr. and Mrs. Kay won numerous Bests in Show with at least half a dozen individual Westies. Their Dreamland Kennels achieved many major successes in the breed, including Top Winning Westie in Canada on numerous occasions.

Fred Fraser has had several notable Best in Show Westies, as have Tom and June Fraser.

Barbara Keenan's Wishing Well Kennels from the United States probably holds the record for Canadian Bests in Show won by Westies with close to a dozen such wins over the years.

Mrs. Daniell-Jenkins and Penny-Belle Storer are well accustomed to the thrill of winning Best in Show with their Westies.

Mrs. Keith Balsdon has gone Best in Show with American and Canadian Champion Winde Mere Gay Gordon. Mrs. Marion Waite has done so with Champion Lymehill's Prockles Picador and American and Canadian Champion Quakertown Quirang. And there have been a number of others whose Westies have thus distinguished themselves.

KENNELS OF THE ROUGE

Kennels of the Rouge was founded in Canada by Mr. and Mrs. J. H.,

Am. and Can. Ch. Winde Mere Gay Gordon, by Am. and Can. Ch. Danny Boy of the Rouge ex Winde Mere Ragamuffin, takes Best in Show and Best Canadian-bred in Show at Aurora Kennel Club 1972. Additionally he took Best in Show and Best Canadian-bred in Show at the United Kennel Club, Montreal, in 1971. He finished his Canadian title at age nine months; won the Manderlay Puppy Challange Trophy in 1965 with a record number of Best Puppy in Group and "in Show" awards. He was bred by Mrs. Keith Balsdon who co-owned this splendid dog with Mrs. Daniell-Jenkins.

Daniell-Jenkins during the year 1948, and was operated over several decades from the Daniell-Jenkins' home in Pickering, Ontario, Canada.

93

Am., Can. and Ber. Ch. Laurie's Piper of the Rouge, by Am. and Can. Ch. Shipmates Hannibal ex Can. Ch. Annie's Memory of the Rouge, was bred by Mr. and Mrs. L. Hunter, and owned by Mrs. Daniell-Jenkins, Kennels of the Rouge. Here he is completing his U.S. title. Much in demand as a stud dog, Piper rivalled his father in siring 70 litters in Canada and the U.S., including 14 champions.

Dorothea Daniell-Jenkins, known also to her friends as Dee, D.J., or Mrs. D.J., started life in South Africa where she remained from her birth until she had reached 16 years age when she left there to attend the Sherborne School for Girls at Sherborne, Dorset, England.

From Sherborne, Dorothea continued her education at St. Hughes College, Oxford University, where she earned a degree in Modern History.

It was while she was living in England that Dorothea met and married John Daniell-Jenkins, this latter event having taken place on June 21, 1934. This was also when Dee discovered Westies, the preferred breed as a pet of John's mother.

John and Dee's daughter, Mary, was born on the family estate at Swansea in Wales. The family, Dorothea, John and Mary, migrated to Canada shortly prior to World War II with their much loved Bullmastiff, Tiger, and leaving behind an equally well-loved Westie, who at age 15 years was probably better off in a familiar home rather than undergoing so drastic a change.

When Tiger died, the Daniell-Jenkins imported a handsome Bullmastiff puppy who became foundation for Kennels of the Rouge, which remains the permanently registered kennel identification with the Canadian Kennel Club.

It was about a year later that Dorothea found herself lonely without a Westie in the house. She set out to find one, at which time she acquired, from Victor Blochin, a son of Rowmore Rabbie and Rowmore Rowmore Rowe, whom they named Bencruachan Tinker in honor of their old dog who had remained in England. This Tinker, eight weeks old when selected, grew up to become a Canadian champion and her show honors included a Reserve Winners at Westminster during the late 1940s, while still a puppy. Tinker had the honor of being not only the first owned in Canada by the Daniell-Jenkins but their first Westie champion as well.

The first stud dog acquired for the Rouge Westie breeding program arrived in 1950 at age three years from Mrs. Finch. This was English,

American and Canadian Champion Shiningcliff Sprig who came from distinguished parentage, sired by English Champion Shiningcliff Simon from Freshnet Folly.

As a show dog, Sprig made his debut at the famed Barrie event where he went from the Open Dog Class to Best of Breed in an unusually strong turnout, then on to First in the Terrier Group. Again from Open Dog Class, he forged through to Best in Show at the Progressive Kennel Club of Canada. The now Canadian Champion Sprig set out to conquer the United States, which he did handily with some significant victories as he became the first of the American champions owned by Dee.

The next important addition to the Kennels of the Rouge Westies was a bitch named Katrine, bred by Frances Parrot, better known in Westie circles as Mrs. Anthony (Polly) Walters. American and Canadian Champion Tyndrum Katrine had been born in 1951, a daughter of American and Canadian Champion Shiningcliff Symmetra Statesman from Rossardon Marie, a descendant of several of the better known Wolvey winners. Katrine was a specialty winner with various other good wins as she gained her titles.

Excitement in the Westie world was high when Florence and Barbara Worcester imported to the U.S. the widely admired great English dog who quickly became English, American and Canadian Champion Cruben Dextor. Dorothea was among those especially admiring of his quality and excellence and she could hardly wait to have something in her own kennel by this son of English Champion Hookwood Mentor. Champion Cruben Dextor's first litter born in the U.S. was from Dee's Rossardon Marie and it included not only Champion Fanfare of the Rouge, who remained with Dee, but also Fons of

Am. and Can. Ch. Dancer's Eminence of the Rouge (Can. Ch. Macdan Emblem of the Rouge ex Am. and Can. Ch. Dancing Hannah of the Rouge); and **Am. and Can. Ch. Denisette Mandan of the Rouge** (Am. and Can. Ch. Danny Boy of the Rouge ex Wigtown Mandy) here are winning Best Brace in Terrier Group at the International K.C. in April 1972. Bred by Mrs. Daniell-Jenkins, owned by Mr. and Mrs. Lorne Gignac, handled by 12-year-old David Gignac. These two also won Best Brace in Show at the Bermuda K.C. in 1972, and at Sackets Harbor, NY in 1971, as well as Best Brace at both CWHWTC and WHWTCA Specialties in 1971.

the Rouge, who was sold to the Shipmates Westies belonging to the Navins.

On the advice of noted breeder Mrs. B. G. Frame, Fantasy was bred to Clairedale Kennel's Champion Clairedale Co-Pilot. Teena of the Rouge from the latter combination also went to Mrs. Navins as another foundation bitch.

Next time around, Fantasy was bred to the Adams' American Canadian Champion Roseneath White Knight, from which litter Dee kept Wendy of the Rouge.

Through Polly Walters, a bitch named Pixie Phebe joined the Westies

Marjadele Schiele with her fabulous Westie brace **Am. and Can. Champions Higgins, and Barley O' The Ridge**. Although well-known winners individually, it is their wins as Brace which have given their owner special pleasure. Included are such victories as Best Brace at the Canadian and Southeast Texas Specialties; plus twice at Montgomery County going on to Best Brace in Show at Montgomery County in 1983, plus an all-breed Best Brace in Show.

Phebe gave the Daniell-Jenkins their Philomel of the Rouge. Both of these Pixie daughters, Meagara and Philomel, were in their own turns to become of special value to the Rouge breeding program.

As the 1950s drew to a close, it was decided by the Daniell-Jenkins that the time had come to phase out the Bullmastiff breeding program in order to increase their Westie activity. Then it was that a male puppy was selected, Wigmac O'My Joshua, carrying through his Wigtown and Rachelwood background strong lines to Champion Cruben Dextor. Also, from

of the Rouge. She was a daughter of Mrs. Walters' famed American Champion Shiningcliff Symmetra Statesman. Bred first to Canadian Champion Shipmates Demos–thenese, a son of Fons ex Teena, Pixie Phebe produced Meagara of the Rouge. Later, in another litter, sired this time by Bencruachan Prince Valiant (grandson of both Champion Cruben Dextor and Champion Shiningcliff Sprig), Pixie

Mrs. Blue, a two-year-old bitch was acquired, Klintilloch Moment, who was a daughter of American Champion Rannoch-Dune Deputy ex Klintilloch Misschief, a Dextor granddaughter who gave Dorothea two of her later stud dogs, American and Canadian Champion Mercury of the Rouge (by Demosthenese) and American and Canadian Champion Danny Boy of the Rouge (by Hannibal).

In 1960 Wendy of the Rouge was bred to Mrs. Frame's American and Canadian Champion Wigtown Talent Scout, from which Dorothea kept Vigil of the Rouge.

John Daniell-Jenkins tragically was killed in a head-on collision while a passenger in the car of a friend on the afternoon of December 4, 1960. Dorothea, who was with him in the car, was also injured but made a good recovery.

After John's death, Dorothea was fortunate in acquiring from Mrs. Navin a most promising two year old, Canadian Champion Shipmates Hannibal, by Roseneath Gay Kilt ex Shipmates Confection. Hannibal was strong in the Dextor lines, his sire being a Dextor great-grandson and his dam both a granddaughter and great-granddaughter of the mighty Dextor. Hannibal was to prove a prepotent sire and become the foundation stud of Dorothea's breeding program through the 1960s-1970s period.

Impressed with Hannibal's qualities, Mrs. Frame (Wigtown), Mrs. McCarty (Mac-a-Dac) and Mrs. Fawcett (Forest Glen) all bred and generously gave to Mrs. D.J. a top bitch puppy from each of these litters as a stud fee. And so in this manner Dorothea acquired what were to become Canadian Champion Wigtown Nightingale, Canadian Champion Mac-a-Dac Rouge Remembrance, and American and Canadian Champion Forest Glen Hannipeg. All three of these bitches went back through their American lines to link with Dextor and Hannibal, back to English Champion Shiningcliff Simon.

During this same period, Dorothea also acquired Cooper's Annie Laurie, a daughter of American Champion Wigtown Talent Scout. She was to prove another invaluable brood bitch.

Gradually receiving requests for puppies from breeders and intending breeders across Canada and the

This was the Top Canadian Westie Bitch for 1985. **Ch. Raglan Ragtime Sophie Tucker** owner-handled by breeder Penny-Belle Scorer, Richmond Hill, Ontario, Canada.

United States, Mrs. D. J. found herself increasing her linebred stock by sometimes supplying a top-quality puppy for part cash and either a puppy back or a litter by lease (in the latter case, the owner receiving part of the proceeds) or limited stud service from a male. Dorothea felt it more important that she help sincere people to get a good start in the breed than it was for her to spend time campaigning once a dog had completed its championship. And it worked out well for her, as it was in this manner that she acquired one of her best stud dogs, American, Canadian, and Bermudian Champion Laurie's Piper of the Rouge, by Hannibal from Canadian Champion Annie's Memory of the Rouge. She also acquired the outstanding bitch American and Canadian Champion Vancot's Rouge Remembrance, by American and Canadian Champion Rannoch Dune Down Beat from Champion Natalie of the Rouge.

When Mrs. Frame was reducing her Wigtowns, in 1969, she gave Wigtown Mandy to Mrs. Daniell-Jenkins. A Down Beat granddaughter, Mandy fit nicely into the breeding program at Rouge, becoming the dam of Canadian and Bermudian Champion Rouge Manabee Zebedeem, a stud dog widely used in Canada and the United States.

After the loss of Mary's older Westie, Dorothea gave her daughter Balsdon Galatea of the Rouge, who combined the Dextor and Shiningcliff lines. When Galatea was bred to Hannibal, Mary in turn gave Dorothea a puppy from the litter who became Canadian Champion Windemere Rouge Midshipman and proved to be another highly satisfactory stud dog. Then Dorothea and Mary co-owned American and Canadian Champion Windemere Gay Gordon—sired by Danny Boy ex a Galatea daughter, Windemere Ragamuffin—who won two Bests in Show and was an excellent sire.

It was during the 1970s that Dorothea obtained two daughters of Mrs. Frame's American Champion Pillerton Prosper (sired by English Champion Pillerton Peterman, a stud dog who had previously proved a useful outcross).

In 1970 Hannibal, then over 11 years of age, sired

Am., Can. and Ber. Ch. Raglan Ragtime Clancy, Am. and Can. C.D. presents a handsome picture of Westie balance and excellence of type. Owned by Penny-Belle Scorer, Clancy was Number One West Highland and Number Five among Terriers as well as Top Winning Westie Puppy in Canada for 1984.

a litter from which Dorothea kept a dog and a bitch. These two became Canadian Champion Junior Hannyin and Judy Hannyin of the Rouge, and their dam was Canadian Champion Jinty of the Rouge, who was out of Vigil, daughter of Wendy, daughter of Fanfare, daughter of Champion Cruben Dextor, thus comprising five generations over a period of 19 years. Jinty was also a great-granddaughter of Champion Shiningcliff Sprig.

At this point, Dorothea had a puppy room with a "Dutch door," the top of which was usually left open so that the puppies were well socialized from birth. With a stock of some 20 Westies, a "retired" veteran dog and bitch were kept always in the house, and they were joined in rotation by usually five or six at a time, so that the dogs all considered themselves to be part of the household—sleeping on their owner's bed, then taking turns in the kennel. Originally designed for Bullmastiffs, the kennel stalls held two Westies with room to spare. Dorothea has always been of the opinion that this freedom provided by the large stalls, with plenty of space for stretching out, and the thirty-foot runs for exercising contributed enormously to the good muscling and strong hindquarters of these little dogs.

She notes that she was always fortunate enough to be able to place dogs and bitches once retired from the show ring and breeding in homes where they lived for many years as much-loved pets.

Having sold the house and ken-

At the important and prestigious Barrie K.C. dog show, one of Canada's leading events, here is **Am. and Can. Ch. Raglan Ragtime Clancy, Am. and Can. C.D.** at age seven months, winning the Group Second in an entry of about 100 terriers, then going on to Fourth place the next day. At these two Barrie events, Clancy was twice Best Puppy in Show and won the all-breed Puppy Sweepstakes which drew 183 entries. Penny-Belle Scorer, owner, Raglan Westies.

nel in 1980, Dorothea Daniell-Jenkins remained a very active member of the dog fancy as a judge who enjoyed tremendous popularity and respect. She appeared on many panels in the United States and Canada each year. The international dog fancy was greatly saddened by the loss of Mrs. D. J. in 1992.

RAGLAN

Raglan West Highland White Terriers is located at Richmond Hill in

Ontario, Canada, where it is owned by Penny-Belle Scorer. Since Westies had been darting in and out of her life as far back as she can remember, it is only natural that she would have some of her own. And so in due course she discussed the subject of the breed with her veterinarians, Dr. John Reeve-Newson and Dr. Martin DeForest, who told her of Mrs. Daniell-Jenkins, "Queen of the Westies," who lived just outside of Toronto at Pickering.

A telephone call led to an invitation to "come see the Westies," and so Penny went to spend a wonderful time looking at and discussing Westies.

Through Dee Daniell-Jenkins, Penny joined the West Highland White Terrier Club of England, whence she received the *English Year Book.* After careful study of the dogs presented there in photo and in pedigree, she decided that she would like to import a Westie bitch from England, from Doris Parr's kennel Arnholme.

Doris Parr had bred Champion Halfmoon of Olac, 1980 Pup of the Year all-breeds and 1981 Top Westie, granddam of the Crufts 1990 Best in Show dog, Champion Olac Moon Pilot. The dam of Half Moon was Arnholme Temporarily Tangerine.

Penny-Belle telephoned England to introduce herself to Doris Parr and tell her about the Raglan Westies. Fortunately, Mrs. Parr did have a bitch that would fill the bill nicely from Tangerine and sired by April Jester, a son of English and American Champion Olac Moon Drift. This youngster had already been shown and qualified for Crufts.

Sweepstakes winner at the Terrier Breeders 1987 Specialty was **Ch. Raglan Fannie Brice** who on that same day also won the Westie Sweepstakes and Best Westie Puppy in Show. Owned and handled by Penny-Belle Scorer, Raglan Kennels. This lovely bitch is a daughter of the Scorers' import, Am., Can. and Bda. Ch. Brierlow Blaze A Trail.

The author loves this photo of **Ch. Raglan Centennial Impudence** who is co-owned by Penny-Belle Scorer and Gerard Livesque. He is the winner of the 1989 Canadian West Highland White Terrier Club Specialty Show. A son of Ch. Brierlow Blaze A Trail.

Several phone calls later, it was agreed that this young bitch, who became Champion Arnholme Almost An Angel, should come to Raglan in Canada. She proved very successful. Almost An Angel (described by Penny-Belle as truly *being* an angel at least in her eyes) is known by the call name "Annie," and is the dam, granddam, or great-granddam of more than 20 champions.

It was about this same period that Penny-Belle's father, Russell Scorer, who had lived in Hawaii, decided that he would like to live permanently in Canada as he enjoyed the Westies so greatly on his annual or semi-annual visits. This was wonderful news for Penny-Belle, who describes her father as being "good company, patient and understanding." So, in 1983, he made the move.

The next Westie to come to Raglan was Stuart. This lovely dog, formally known as American and Canadian Champion Biljon Bisbee of Nollcrest, gained his Canadian title in one weekend, then went on to become Canada's Number Two

At age seven and one half months **Am., Can., and Ber. Ch. Brierlow Blaze A Trail** completed his Canadian title in two weekends. Number One Westie in Canada for 1988; Number Four Terrier. Owned by Raglan Kennels, Penny-Belle Scorer, Richmond Hill, Ontario, Canada.

Am. and Can. Ch. Biljon Bisbee of Nollcrest gained his Canadian's Number Two Westie; Number Five Terrier in 1984. Owned by Raglan Westies.

Westie and Number Five Terrier for 1984.

The next big winner was a homebred named "Clancy," who was a son of Stuart and Annie. At seven-and-a-half months of age, Clancy gained his Canadian championship at the Barrie shows with a Group Second and a Group Fourth, with over one hundred terriers entered each day; plus he also gained the Puppy Sweepstakes in which 183 puppies representing all breeds competed; and he was Best Terrier Puppy and Best Puppy in Show, too. Quite a smashing start for a young fellow!

Clancy went on to become Canada's Number One Westie Puppy of 1984; Number One Westie and Number Five Terrier in 1985; then, in 1986, Clancy gained his C.D. in Canada and in the United States. Clancy's full name is American and Canadian Champion Raglan Ragtime Clancy, American and Canadian C.D.

In 1985 Penny-Belle learned from Doris Parr about an outstanding Westie dog, Brierlow Blaze A Trail, bred by Janet Bowden in England, with Arnholme on the dam's side. The Scorers decided to purchase this dog and now co-own him. By the age of 15 months, "Bobby," as he was known, gained his American, Canadian, and Bermudian championships, and his name had now become a very famous one in the world of Westies.

American, Canadian and Bermudian Champion Brierlow Blaze A Trail was a tremendous asset to Raglan Kennels as a sire, as a show dog, and as a member of their Westie family.

Bobby became Canada's Number One Westie for 1986, 1987, and 1988; while among All Terriers he was rated Number Nine in 1986; Number Three in 1987; and Number Four Terrier for 1988. In 1986 he was also Number One Westie puppy, making him the first ever to gain both Number One Westie Puppy and Number One Westie in the same year.

Penny-Belle points out that she has been extremely selective in her breeding program and opts to linebreed her dogs. When occasionally, as happens to us all, it becomes necessary to use a Westie of a different line, the selection is made with utmost care with attention paid to the type similar to that of her own dogs. Wisely, she has never bred to a dog on that dog's winning record, but rather intently studies the pedigrees for three or four generations

Am., Can. and Bda. Ch. Brierlow Blaze A Trail with owner Penny-Belle Scorer and handler Bob Whitney. Honors won by this dog include those of Canada's Number One Westie in 1986 and Number One Puppy. Plus Number One Westie in 1987 and 1988 along with Number Three and Number Four Terrier respectively.

back. She then bases her selection on this information, which she feels best leads her to the correct choice. Certainly her beliefs and practices have met with notable success for there have been more than 30 Raglan champions bred or owned by this enthusiast.

Penny-Belle has some very definite ideas about the responsibilities

Am. and Can. Ch. Raglan Ragtime Pearl Bailey is the dam of no less than five well-known winners: Ch. Raglan Ragtime Sophie Tucker, Ch. Raglan Jypsi Rosi, Ch. Raglan Fanny Brice, Ch. Raglan Pearl of Impudence, and Am. and Can. Ch. Raglan Ragtime Robbie. Owned by Raglan Westies, Penny-Belle Scorer.

been provided; and she prefers that they live as family dogs where they and their new owners share a mutual association. Also she will not let them go where the new owners fail to provide a sturdy crate and, in the case of a puppy, a playpen in which the youngster can safely amuse itself away from harm when left alone. As she explains to the new owners, a puppy left unattended for even a 15-minute period can do more damage to our possessions and perhaps harm to itself than the mere cost of a puppy pen.

Pet Westies from Raglan all are sold on the Canadian Kennel Club Non-Breeding Agreement, with the understanding that such puppies (or mature dogs) must be spayed or neutered. Proper attention to the dog's safety is also essential, such as the dog's being walked on a lead when outdoors and never being turned loose other than in its fenced yard. There are too many dangers waiting to overtake dogs not protected in this manner.

of a breeder in placement of both puppies and adult Westies in order to assure that each is placed in the finest and most appreciative of homes. She would never take pride in a dog's show wins or breeding success if, in accomplishing them, the happiness and well being of the dog were sacrificed. In placing her dogs, she would never permit one to be placed where no fenced yard had

The thing we admire most of all about Penny-Belle's attitude towards her puppies and grown dogs, however, is the one demanding that no dog or puppy purchased *ever* may change hands without her approval of the situation. To which we

Penny-Belle Scorer with her **Ch. Raglan Jypsi Rosi** taking Best of Breed at Credit Valley.

say, "Bravo," knowing of supposedly reputable breeders who, once they have sold a dog, completely wash their hands of it and refuse to lend assistance should the purchaser have to re-locate or resign ownership. Penny-Belle is adamant in her belief that such situations should be of deep concern to breeders, who owe it to their dogs never to abandon them and always to demand that they must not change hands without her knowledge and consent.

The Storers are the type of folk who like having their dogs as family members, and many years ago the decision was reached that the Westies would be kept in the house. Thus when their latest house was built it was done so with a split rear level and set on the side of a hill providing for lots of canine exercise. Nearly an acre of the 30 acres of land has been fenced in for the dogs; plus half of the lower level provides their play room where the males and females can run and play together. It speaks well of Westie temperament and of the way these dogs are kept that three males run with each other at all times. Their

Am. and Can. Ch. Sno-Bilt's Pac Man. Bred by Jodine Vertuno, Naperville, IL.

owner has discovered over the years that the only time any aggression occurs is when one puts a leash on them and then faces them off. This is, of course, the common sparring method that has been used to make terriers aggressive.

The dog's play room has a grooming area, laundry facilities, and a mini-kitchen, with many places to sit or curl up. They also have their own T.V., and it is fun to watch them watch it!

Westies in Australia

West Highland White Terriers have been in Australia over a considerable period of time. Indeed some say that the breed was in that country in the early 1900s. Little was done about it though until following World War II, when some dogs were interchanged between Australia and New Zealand.

It was during the 1960s, mostly in New South Wales, that the Westies began making their presence known. The West Highland White Terrier Club of Australia was organized in New South Wales during September 1963, the first in that country. Headquartered at Sydney, its membership quickly attracted fanciers from Victoria, South Australia and Queensland, as well as New Zealand. Their inaugural show took place on November 15, 1964, and the club proudly accepted a handsome trophy given by the West Highland White Terrier Club of Illinois in tribute to what was taking place among

This is an Australian import owned by Mrs. Eileen McNulty, Java Center, NY, taking a Winners Dog, owner-handled at Montgomery County. **Am. and Aust. Ch. MacPrain Machoman,** by Aust. and New Zeal. Ch. Wistmill Woodpecker of Whitebriar ex Whitebriar Jillaroo. He was bred by Mrs. L.A. Donohue and registered in the U.S. by Mrs. McNulty in April 1986.

Westie friends "Down Under."

The winner of this first Australian West Highland White Terrier specialty was an import from England, Champion Busybody of Branston, daughter of English Champion Sollershot Sun Up ex English Champion Brindie of Branston, bred by Mrs. D. M. Dennis, born in 1961. Wolvey Puritan won the dog Challenge Certificate at this event, he, too, an English importation. Mr. R. Burnell of Sydney judged this first specialty show.

In 1965 the club's second specialty took place under judge Mr. F. Luland, also from Sydney. Best in Show was a repeat of the previous year's winner. English Champion Busybody of Branston, who also scored the additional distinction of having been the dam of the dog who won the C.C. for his sex, Langsyne Philabeg.

During the 1960s some splendid dogs representing the cream of British bloodlines were brought from England to Australia where they were used advantageously in various breeding programs establishing the background for some excellent Australian homebreds. Notable among them were Pollyann of Paterscourt and Wolvey Provest, brought in by Peter Brown as additions to his Peteraffles Kennels in Goulburn. Also two bitches, Famecheck Delibes and Famecheck Nimble.

Also around this same period Mrs. McEachern brought Wolvey Puritan to Wagga. For her Langsyne Westies, Miss B. Faulk selected and brought over two very nice Branstons, Baxter and English Champion Busybody, along with Famecheck Serenade.

Southern Australia had the Pilelo Westies, owned by Phil Cunningham, where numbered among the assets were such sterling imports as English Champion Buttons of Helmsley, Famecheck Lucrative, and Stonygap Freddie.

The 1980s found Australia with some

Ch. Whitebriar Jaymandie, by Ch. Whitebriar Jimmick ex Ch. Whitebriar Jillsown, was bred in England by Jean Johnson and owned in the United States by Helene and Seymour Weiss. She is completing her championship as Best of Winners at the West Highland White Terrier Club under Mrs. J.H. Daniell-Jenkins, owner of the famed Rouge Westies. Handler, William Ferrara.

splendid Westies and highly enthusiastic fanciers working towards their breed's future. J.H. and Mrs. R. Roche, at Tahmoor in New South Wales, are among those with notable Westies, theirs including some splendid representatives of the breed such as Australian Champion Macsped Beau Geste (Australian, English and New Zealand Champion Japple of Whitebriar, an import from the United Kingdom, ex Australian Champion Chatine Snow Maiden) who was born in 1982. Also Australian Champion MacPrain Magician (Australian Champion MacPrain Moonraker ex Australian Champion MacPrain Magic Moments) who was born in 1981.

of Australian Champion MacPrain Macho Man, sired by Australian and New Zealand Champion

Ch. Whitebriar Jollimont taking a good Group placement for owner Eve Varley at Land O' Lakes K.C. in June 1987. Dora Lee Wilson handling. Jollimont, by Jaimont of Whitebriar ex Jollity of Whitebriar, is a grandson of Eng. and N.Z. Ch. Domaroy Saraband of Whitebriar. He represents some half-dozen generations of Whitebriar breeding.

Mrs. L. A. Donahue at Catherine Field, New South Wales, has a notable producing bitch in her kennel representing the finest of the impressive Whitebriar strain from England, which is now very popular in Australia. The bitch to whom I refer is Whitebriar Jillaroo, daughter of English, Australian and New Zealand Champion Japple of Whitebriar, from the U.K., ex New Zealand Champion Whitebriar Jixey.

Among others, Jillaroo is the dam

Wistmill Woodpecker imported to America from Australia by Mrs. Evelyn McNulty of Jave, New York.

Mrs. Donahue also co-owns, with Miss M. Murphy, Australian Champion Wistmill Woodpecker of Whitebriar, imported from the U.K., by English Champion Kilbrannon Crispin ex English Champion Whitebriar Jillsown. Woodpecker was born in 1982.

Miss Murphy herself is the owner of several impressive Westies, including English and Australian Champion Strathtay Viking at Domaroy, born in 1978, by English Champion Domaroy Saracen; plus

109

At the Scottish Breeds Canine Club Championship Show for 1990, Irish and Annual Ch. for 1989, **Glenveagh Gabriella**, homebred and owned by Mrs. Johnston of Ireland, who poses proudly following winning Best in Show.

bitches Champion Whitebriar Joyce and Champion Glen Atwel Galaxy.

Mrs. A. Moon owns Champion Arapala Alabaster, born in 1981, by Champion MacPrain Moonraker ex Champion MacPrain Marisa, and Australian Champion Arapala Annsolome, born in 1983, by Australian Champion Wistmill Woodpecker of Whitebriar ex Australian Champion MacPrain Marisa.

To Mrs. J. Welson belongs a highly successful dog, English, Australian, and New Zealand Champion Domaroy Saraband of Whitebriar. Born in England in 1976, this is a son of English Champion Tasman March of Time from English Champion Domaroy Erisort Serenade. He is the sire of champions and very widely admired.

Friends who have visited Australia during recent years comment that the Westies are in good hands. Surely the future should be successful for the little White Highlanders "Down Under" in keeping with their progress of the past.

Becoming Acquainted with the Breed

Many of you who read this book will do so owing to having simply met a single West Highland White Terrier. As fondness and acquaintance have increased, you find yourself gradually feeling that this is *the* breed of dog for you, and now plan for a deeper involvement—perhaps as an owner, a breeder, an exhibitor or even eventually as a judge. As all this strikes you, so does the fact that you must know *everything* about this breed—its early history and current status, a true understanding of the dogs and their original purpose, their ideal physical

Ch. Principal's MacGyver, by Ch. Holyrood's Hot Shot ex Elsinore Plupurrfect O'Malley, bred by Karen R. Polizzo and owned by Robert and Susan M. Ernst.

appearance, and much more.

At this point in time, knowledge and understanding of the standard of the breed should become the newcomer's target: no one can be considered truly knowledgeable of a breed unless the words of the standard are not simply familiar but resolutely *understood*. A parrot-like recitation of the standard, in other words, is of little value to anyone who is unable to interpret the words and mentally picture exactly what is being described.

Breed standards have their roots far back in the sands of time and, almost without exception, originate in the country of the dogs' origin

Clancy was all groomed and ready to go to the dog show when he was let out for just one brief moment, and now look! Penny-Belle Scorer is Clancy's patient owner.

and the locale of the earliest planned breedings. In the beginning, they were simple descriptions of the dog's necessary traits to do a good day's work and the physical features that made him compatible for the job. As time progressed, the appearance of the dog took a larger share of importance; and finally it has come down to the dog's physical appearance or good looks edging a bit ahead of

working proficiency.

Fortunately, Westies are among the breeds where the original instincts still remain and can be developed quickly with encouragement, as proved in working trials. But why would this *not* be the case since no drastic changes in the Westie have taken place that might diminish these talents?

All Westie historians, whose words we have read in speaking of the standard, comment on the fact that very little change in the breed has taken place since its first recognition in Great Britain and point to the first official standard in 1909.

Over the years, one area of the standard has been changed: the desired height at the withers was originally described as 8–12 inches, which many felt allowed for too wide a range in this area. In 1948, a combined committee meeting of the Scottish Club (the first active in the breed) and the English Westie Club (founded in 1906) was called specifically to discuss the size issue. The committee determined that "about 11 inches" for dogs would best suffice. Also the weight limit effective until that time (14–18 pounds for dogs, two pounds less for bitches) was deleted. We assume that this was due to a feeling that this further requirement was superfluous; although occasionally someone

Ch. Kilkerran 'N Wicket A Kut Above has many successes to his credit. A very outstanding sideview which correctly presents balance and quality. Note short, level back, proper tail set, body, and other characteristics for which we seek in judging.

does rise up and lament the fact that the weight ratio to size was helpful.

The interpretation of the color section of the standard has changed somewhat, although the words are actually the same. Obviously, it has always been intended that the West Highland White Terrier be a *white* dog, since "White" is his middle name. At the beginning of the 20th century, a white dog often bore traces of yellowish or sand-like tinges in the coat, especially down the center of the back. Such a dog for many years was considerd to be a white dog. Not any more, however! For a number of years now pure white means exactly that—truly *white*, not tinged or streaked in any manner. And the dog with whom you hope to win, or plan to use for breeding, must be a clear and sparkling white.

When you bring your Westie into the show ring, the first features which will strike the judge are over-all balance (all parts of the dog looking in correct ratio to each other). The head then takes the eye: this magnificent and beautiful head, face framed with snow white whiskers, is really the trademark of the breed. Combined with a short back, correct length of neck, correct front and rear, one is looking at a most distinctive little dog. Handsome and a joy to own, these little dogs sparkle

113

Riverside's Bonnie Jacinda, one of the outstanding West Highland White Terriers owned by Eve Varley, Wichita, KS.

with personality, their "ready-for-anything" attitude is most endearing.

On the following pages you will find the American standard of the breed for West Highland White Terriers. The requirements for the breed in England, Canada and the United States are basically the same and sufficiently similar to call for an evenness of type throughout the Westie world. The standard is not to be read a few times then tucked away, never again to see the light of day. It should be referred to regularly and frequently. Read, re-read, and consider what the words are saying as you do so. Especially read the standard thoughtfully both before and after dog shows, as this will sharpen your wits to really notice what takes place within the ring.

The more familiar you become with the standard, the more you will really see the dog, as you realize the reason for the various requirements. Of course, his color distinguishes his breed from all other terriers. Then, think of the dog's early history, the tasks that he performed, and realize that correctly his conformation should be compatible with these words and occupations. Whether or not your Westie is ever called upon to "go to ground" or to dispatch vermin, or fight a fox or badger, he should be physically equipped in temperament and conformation to do so. Those strong jaws with their big teeth; solid, chesty body; conformation for reach of forequarters and drive from behind; and quality of coat are there for a *reason*, as are his smallness of build, sturdiness, and forelegs built for digging. When you have thoroughly understood why all these attributes are important, then you will truly have learned what is wanted, needed and required in an admirable West Highland White Terrier.

AMERICAN STANDARD FOR THE WEST HIGHLAND WHITE TERRIER

The standard of the breed, to which one hears and reads such frequent reference, is the guide to those who are interested in breeding, showing, judging, or just plain becoming acquainted with a specific breed of dog. It outlines, in great detail, each and every feature of that breed, both its physical characteristics and its temperament; it accurately describes the dog from whisker to tail, creating a clear impression of what is to be considered correct and incorrect, the features comprising "breed type," and the probable temperament and

FCI. Int., Am., Can., Ber., and Mex., Ch. Skaket's Candy Man, C.D.X., T.D., C.G., T.T. winning Best of Breed at Montgomery County 1988 from the Veterans Class, then on to second in the Group. This notable dog was bred and is owned by Nancy and Mitzi Gauthier.

behavior pattern of typical members of the breed.

It is the standard which is used by breeders endeavoring to produce dogs of quality for the show ring. It is the tool with which judges evaluate the dogs before them in the show ring. It draws for the new fancier a word picture of what breeders and judges are, or should be, seeking.

It tells what is ideal in the breed, and what is not. What is beautiful, adding up to correct type, and what equips the dog to fulfill the purposes for which its breed was originally developed. It is the result of many patient hours spent in study and research, and in dedicated work by fanciers with the breed's best interests at heart.

Our present standards represent the best of the earlier ones, combined occasionally with modification or clarification to make for better understanding. They are carefully thought out to provide the utmost protection of the breed, and comprehension of what they are telling us is essential for our own true appreciation of these dogs.

The current West Highland White Terrier Club of America standard for the breed was approved by the American Kennel Club on December 13, 1988, and became effective on February 1, 1989.

GENERAL APPEARANCE: The West Highland White Terrier is a small, game, well-balanced, hardy-looking terrier, exhibiting good showmanship, possessed with no small amount of self-esteem, strongly built, deep in chest and back ribs, with a straight back and powerful hindquarters on muscular legs, and exhibiting in marked degree a great combination of strength and activity. The coat is about two inches long, white in color, hard, with plenty of soft undercoat. The dog should be neatly presented, the longer coat on the back and sides trimmed to blend into the shorter neck and shoulder coat. Considerable hair is left around the head to act

Ch. Round Town Ivan the Terror, a multi-Group and Best in Show winner of 1991–92. Owners Mr. and Mrs. R.D. Musser, Mackinac Island, MI. Ivan is handled by George Ward and the judge is Anna Katherine Nicholas.

Ch. Orions Rising Sun, by Ch. Cynosure Orion the Hunter ex Ch. Orions Altair. Owned by Ida Keushgenian and Ed Curran; bred by Orion Kennels and Ida and Joe Keushgenian. Pictured taking Best in Sweepstakes at Westbury, NY in October 1989. Judge is Mrs. Lois Hallmark.

present a round appearance from the front. Should be in proportion to the body.

Expression—Piercing, inquisitive, pert.

Eyes—Widely set apart, medium in size, almond-shaped, dark brown in color, deep set, sharp and intelligent. Looking from under heavy eyebrows, they give a piercing look. Eye rims are black.

Faults—Small, full or light-colored eyes. **Ears**—Small, carried tightly erect, set wide apart, on the top outer edge of the skull. They terminate in a sharp point, and must never be cropped. The

as a frame for the face to yield a typical Westie expression.

SIZE, PROPORTION, SUBSTANCE: The ideal size is 11 inches at the withers for dogs and ten inches for bitches. A slight deviation is acceptable. The Westie is a compact dog with good balance and substance. The body between the withers and the root of the tail is slightly shorter than the height at the withers. Short-coupled and well-boned. **Faults:** Over or under height limits. Fine-boned.

HEAD: Shaped to

All the way to the top, **Ch. Mac-Ken-Char's Irish Navigator** is here winning Best in Show at Lackawanna Kennel Club in 1985. Jaimi Glodek, handling, and Joanne Glodek, breeders-owners. This is the top-winning Westie sire of all time with at least 85 champions to his credit.

hair on the ears is trimmed short and is smooth and velvety, free of fringe at the tips. Black skin pigmentation is preferred. **Faults**—Round-pointed, broad, large ears set closely together, not held tightly erect, or placed too low on the side of the head. **Skull**—Broad, slightly longer than the muzzle, not flat on top but slightly domed between the ears. It gradually tapers to the eyes. There is a definite stop, eyebrows are heavy. **Faults**—Long or narrow skull. **Muzzle**—Blunt, slightly shorter than the skull, powerful and gradually tapering to the nose, which is large and black. The jaws are level and powerful. Lip pigment is black. **Faults**—Muzzle longer than skull. Nose color other than black. **Bite**—The teeth are large for the size of the dog. There must be six incisor teeth between the canines of both lower and upper jaws. An occasional missing premolar is acceptable. A tight scissors bite with upper incisors slightly overlapping the lower incisors or level mouth is equally acceptable. **Faults**—Teeth defective or misaligned. Any incisors missing, or several premolars missing. Teeth overshot or undershot.

NECK, TOPLINE, BODY: Neck—Muscular and well set on sloping shoulders. The length of neck should be in proportion to the remainder of the dog. **Faults**—Neck too long or too short. **Topline**—Flat and level, both standing and moving. **Faults**—High rear, any deviation from above. **Body**—Compact and of good substance. Ribs deep and well arched in the upper half of rib, extending at least to the elbows, and presenting a flattish side appearance. Back ribs of considerable depth, and distance from last rib to upper thigh as short as compatible with free movement of the body. Chest very deep and extending to the elbows, with breadth in proportion to the size of the dog. Loin short, broad and strong. **Faults**—Back weak, either too long or too short. Barrel ribs, ribs above elbows. **Tail**—Relatively short, with good substance, and shaped like a

Co-owner Jaimi Glodek with judge Ron Krohne who has just awarded Best of Winners at Trenton K.C. in 1987 to **Ch. Glengidge Moxie Mac-Ken-Char** owned by Jaimi and her mother, Joanne Glodek. Helene and Seymour Weiss are the breeders of this splendid little dog.

A stunning portrait of the renowned Best in Show winning **Ch. Pagan Ghost,** one of the "stars" from the Shelburne Kennels of Mr. and Mrs. George Seemann, Jr., South Norwalk, CT. A wonderful representation of the type, balance and quality that add up to a correct Westie.

carrot. When standing erect it is never extended above the top of the skull. It is covered with hard hair without feather, as straight as possible, carried gaily but not curled over the back. The tail is set on high enough so that the spine does not slope down to it. The tail is never docked. *Faults*—Set too low, long, thin, carried at half mast or curled over back.

FOREQUARTERS: Angulation, Shoulders—Shoulder blades are well laid back and well knit at the backbone. The shoulder blade should attach to an upper arm of moderate length, and sufficient angle to allow for definite body overhang. *Faults*—Steep or loaded shoulders. Upper arm too short or too straight. **Legs**—Forelegs are muscular and well boned, relatively short, but with sufficient length to set the dog up so as not to be too close to the ground. The legs are reasonably straight, and thickly covered with short, hard hair. They are set in under the shoulder blades with definite body overhang before them. Height from elbow to withers and elbow to ground should be approximately the same. **Faults**—Out at elbows, light bones, fiddle front. **Feet**—Forefeet are larger than the hind ones, are round, proportionate in size, strong, thickly padded; they may properly be turned out slightly. Dewclaws may be removed. Black pigmentation is most desirable on pads of all feet and nails, although nails may lose coloration in older dogs.

HINDQUARTERS: Angulation—Thighs are very muscular, well angulated, not set wide apart, with hock well bent, short, and parallel when viewed from the rear. **Legs**—Rear legs are muscular and relatively short and sinewy. **Faults**—Weak hocks, long hocks, lack of angulation. Cow hocks. **Feet**—Hind feet are smaller than front feet, and are thickly padded. Dewclaws may be removed.

COAT: Very important and seldom seen to perfection. Must be double-coated. The head is shaped by plucking the hair to present the round appearance. The outer coat consists of straight, hard white hair, about two inches long, with shorter coat on neck and shoulders, properly blended and trimmed to blend shorter areas into furnishings, which are longer on stomach and legs. The ideal coat is hard, straight and white, but a hard straight coat that may have some wheaten tipping is preferable to a white fluffy or soft coat. Furnishings may be somewhat softer and longer but should never give the appearance of fluff. **Faults**—Soft coat. Any silkiness or tendency to curl. Any open or single coat, or one which is too short.

COLOR: The color is white, as defined by the breed's name. **Faults**—Any coat color other than white. Heavy wheaten color.

GAIT: Free, straight and easy all around. It is a distinctive gait, not stilted, but powerful, with reach and drive. In front the leg is freely extended forward by the shoulder. When seen from the front the legs do not move square, but tend to move toward the center of gravity. The hind movement is free, strong and fairly close. The hocks are freely flexed and drawn close under the body, so that when moving off the foot the body is thrown or pushed forward with some force. Overall ability to move is usually best evaluated from the side, and topline remains level. **Faults**—Lack of reach in front, and/or drive behind. Stiff, stilted or too wide movement.

TEMPERAMENT: Alert, gay, courageous and self-reliant, but friendly. **Faults**—Excess timidity or excess pugnacity.

In the ring at Montgomery 1988. **Ch. Skaket's Candy Man, C.D.X., T.D.** stepping out nicely for Mary Gauthier and Mitzi Gauthier.

Your Well-Groomed Westie

A dog with so much potential for handsome beauty as a Westie is one especially deserving of good grooming. Particularly when one considers that it is really not all that difficult to keep a member of this breed tidied up and neat, as compared to the hours which must be used grooming other popular breeds.

His being a small dog, the area to be groomed on a Westie is well within reason—no excuse for weariness here! Of course, the non-show-dog Westie needs little other than brushing, combing, and a small amount of tidying (preferably done by plucking with your hand as I will explain, and by snipping off rough ends which have grown scraggly and look untidy).

But what about bathing, since he is a white dog—I can just hear my readers protest! And here is where

Best in Show **Am. and Ber. Ch. Mac-Ken-Char's Irish Navigator** is showing off his well-groomed coat. Bred, owned and handled by Joanne and Jaime Glodek. This is how your Westie should look at show time.

you get more good news, as the frequent bathing of a Westie is the very worst thing you possibly can do for his coat, which takes its beauty from consisting of outercoat hairs which are *hard*, about two inches long, and straight. Obviously since shampooing

121

softens hair texture and can encourage a tendency to curl, this is not the way to go with a Westie!

So save bathing for real emergencies which can only be handled in this manner. An encounter with a skunk (for which the remedy is dousing with tomato juice which then must be shampooed out) or another drastic occurrence should be your sole reason for resorting to the soap-and-water method.

GROOMING ESSENTIALS

A brush, some combs, stripping tool, scissors, nail clippers, and a nail file are the basic essentials with which to groom a West Highland. To do the job properly, the dog should be stood on a table (this is not a breed to groom in your lap). The best kind for this purpose is a rubber-topped folding professional grooming table with adjustable height for you to work comfortably either standing or sitting, as you prefer. Such grooming tables fold flat when not in use for easy storage or convenience in travelling. The grooved rubber top gives the dog a feeling of security as his feet will not be likely to slip, and they can be equipped with an upright "arm" to which one attaches a noose for collaring the dog, eliminating the possibility of his sudden exit should the mood strike him.

The tools you purchase should be carefully selected and of high quality. Cheap grooming items are never a bargain, as the best available will not only do a better job but last longer as well. The necessities are the finest brush you can find, either pure bristle (the best of which are generally made in England) or a high quality wire brush, the wires being set in rubber. Either will work well for you, so select the one with which you feel most comfortable and pleased.

Other necessities for a well-groomed Westie are a fairly coarse-toothed metal comb to go over the

Ch. Wee Mack's Heavy on the Mister by Ch. Whitebriar Jacksprat ex Wee Mack's Nitty Gritty is finishing the title with this "major" win handled by Susan McNulty, the daughter of owner Mrs. Eileen McNulty, Java, NY.

Ch. Kilkerran 'N Wicket A Kut Above, by Haweswalton Man About Town ex Ch. Kilkerran Lady Guinevere. Bred by Vicki Beets and Kathy Kompare. Owners are Nancy Spelke, Laura Moreno and Kathy Kompare.

coat thoroughly once the brushing has been completed. You will also need two stripping knives, a coarse one and a fine one; thinning shears; and very excellent scissors with, if you like, blunt rounded tips to assure against accidents, these being used for tidying up scragglers and any hairs spoiling the appearance of a smooth outline. Each of these have their own special role to play in the appearance of your Westie, thus each is of importance. You must learn when and how to use each as you practice grooming.

Also important are a good pair of nail clippers, sturdy and well made, for cutting the nails, which dogs

Bergit Cody giving a grooming lesson for Westie owners at a seminar in Langley, B.C., Canada. The McDonalds travelled hundreds of miles from their home in Oregon to attend this event.

wherever you keep the grooming tools.

Even family Westies should be thoroughly brushed and combed twice weekly. Place yours on the grooming table, noose comfortably in the correct position around his neck, and start work with your brush. At the top of the neck, always brush and comb the Westie coat in the direction it naturally lies. Never do a Westie in reverse. Every move should be geared towards the fact that Westie hair lies down, top coat on top of under-coat, and all your work on it should be directed towards encouraging this to be the case. Another part of grooming is the teeth. They should be checked regularly and tartar, if present, removed with a tooth scraper.

The mature Westie wears a double coat, the outer one being the one which requires work. This outer coat ideally is about two inches long, in some cases going as much as an inch beyond that; should be hard in texture (the more so the more desirable), with shorter coat covering and blending in at the neck and shoulders.

Beneath this is the undercoat, which consists of short hair of a texture similar to cotton which forms, thick and close, a splendid protective covering foundation for the long, hard hairs of the outercoat.

It is on the outercoat that we work most diligently. This grows in a cycle which culminates in the little dog doing what is known as "blowing

usually detest. This should be done on a weekly basis as it is easier to *not* let them go too long until the quick has grown down too far, making it almost impossible to shorten the nail without painfully cutting into it. Aim to take just the tip of the nail each time (avoiding the pinkish line running down the center of the nail which is the quick). If you cut into the quick, that nail will bleed and may be sensitive for a day or two. Bleeding can be stopped with a dab of styptic powder which should at all times be in the tack box or one's coat." As the hairs reach their greatest length, 2–3 inches, as we have already noted, each dies off and must be pulled out to make way for a fresh brand new coat. This is where hand plucking comes in, the standby of the long-time well-experienced terrier men and women, done by grasping each hair (or a small clump of them) firmly between the thumb and forefinger and pulling with a short, quick jerk. Do not be fearful of doing this, as it is painless to the dog and the ideal manner in which to clear away dead coat. This should be continued over several days if necessary, until all traces of the dead, dull hair are gone. Then very quickly you will note a new top coat appearing. While a Westie puppy matures, the youngster's coat may range from soft to quite hard. This hardness can best be encouraged by early stripping.

When you start to brush your Westie, do so most carefully, watching as you proceed for any sign of "hot spots," fleas or flea eggs, knots, tangles, or any other conditions which may lead to problems unless treated promptly and appropriately. If you are not accustomed to handling them yourself, consult your

Best of Opposite Sex in Sweepstakes at 1988 WHWTC of Greater Baltimore. Best in Sweeps, Reserve Winners Bitch in 1988 and Reserve Winners Bitch 1989 at WHWTC of S.E. Michigan. This is **Dawn's Pard'n Me Boys** by Am. and Can. Ch. Dawn's Up 'N' Adam, Am. and Can. C.D.X., C.G., ex Am. and Can. Ch. Dawn's Rise 'n' Shine. Breeder, Dawn L. Martin. Owners, Patricia H. Marks and Dawn L. Martin. Dawn's Highland Scots, Saylorsburg, PA.

veterinarian or your dog's breeder or the pet supplier with regard to treatment for the skin and/or insects. Knots and tangles should be worked out if possible *(only cut these when all else has failed),* doing so with your fingers and gently with the comb. Watch, too, for clumps of loose hair which may be waiting to be plucked out.

Remember that the brushing has not been completed until the legs, chest and under areas, and tail have had their share, too.

When the brush has been used thoroughly and with care, combing time has arrived. Your wide-toothed metal comb is the one for this, and it should be carefully and gently used wherever the brush has already been, in order to complete the job.

Final attention is paid to the head. Whiskers should be combed forward and wide at the sides; upward and forward on top of the head making them act as a frame for the head and face, which is a most pleasing aspect of the Westie's general appearance.

When it comes to trimming your Westie, it is my opinion that nothing can take the place of your watching it done by an expert, either the breeder who sold you the puppy or dog, a friend who has raised them for awhile, or a terrier handler you know. You may take the dog to a professional groomer or handler to learn how it is done, of course, for a fee as the capable professionals are hard-pressed for time. It would be well worth your while, though, to learn how the experts do it, espe-

cially if you are planning to show the dog yourself. Doing up a terrier correctly is very definitely a *talent,* and does not come easy to everyone.

Never under any circumstances allow anyone to use hair clippers on

A busy day at Montgomery County some years back with handler George Ward. Being groomed with a last minute touch up before the judging takes place, under George's expert hands, is **Ch. Round Town Duke J. Ellington;** while waiting her turn on the other grooming table is **Ch. Round Town Ella J. Fitzgerald.** Ella, who was Best of Opposite Sex that day, several years later gained permanent possession of the Rouge Trophy for Best of Opposite Sex which needed several such wins to do so. These two superb Westies are breeder-owned by Dan and Amelia Musser, Round Town Kennels, who divide their time between Lainesburg and Mackinac, MI.

BATHING TIPS

Having advised you to avoid bathing your Westie whenever possible, we shall nevertheless make a few suggestions for those times when doing so seems unavoidable. Sometimes the underneath and legs may become soiled or muddy, necessitating a bath or "clean up" with a damp towel or "dry shampoo."

Before starting with the bath, place a drop of castor oil in each eye to prevent soap irritation, and a wad of cotton in each ear to prevent water or suds entering the ear canal. Using tepid water and a shampoo spray, wet the dog down with a mild shampoo made expressly for dogs available in your pet-supply center.

Lather the dog only once, always rinsing thoroughly with particular care as you want no traces of soap left behind. Soap residue can cause irritation and itching, which may lead eventually to skin problems.

The whiskers on the head and face should be carefully cleaned with a wet washcloth.

When the dog is clean and thoroughly rinsed, place him on the table and blot out the excess moisture with turkish towels. You may wish to use a hair dryer on *low*, blowing with the lay of the hair so that it will dry lying flat; or you may place a large folded turkish towel around the dog completely covering him from his head back and pin it with large safety pins under the chin, behind the forelegs and further back to hold the towel in place keeping the hair flat, making sure that the towel is fitting snugly.

Believe is or not, this truly is **Am. and Can. Ch. Raglan Ragtime Pearl Bailey** displaying the after-effects of gardening. Restoring this Westie's coat to its usual pristine whiteness must have indeed taken a bit of doing. One of the famous Westies at Raglan Kennels.

your Westie's coat which may never again return, thus your dog's appearance is ruined along with any chance for success in the show ring.

If you find that hand-stripping presents a problem for you, then learn to use a stripping knife for removal of dead hair when "blowing of the coat" gets under way. This will perhaps be easier for you to manage, and even though the results are liable to be less professional in appearance than when hand-plucking is used, they will often suffice.

If you have a problem with hand plucking, you may find it helpful to rub your thumb and forefinger over grooming chalk which should enable you to get a firmer grip.

If your Westie is a family dog, you will probably have no trouble doing the needed trimming yourself for a neat and cared-for appearance. When you comb out the whiskers, inspect them for longer or scraggly hairs which spoil the outline, then carefully even them off with your scissors. The many photos of outstanding Westies illustrating this book should be carefully studied as they present an eloquent statement of how the mature Westie should look at the various stages of development along the way.

recognized breeder of show-type Westies is the guidance this breeder can give you, and gladly will, when you are preparing to show a dog from the kennel. Naturally they want to see it succeed as its championship and other wins are a credit to the breeder. So do not hesitate to ask for advice along the way as show time for the puppy nears. I am a firm believer that something as important as correct coat care for show dogs should not be learned

Am. and Mex. Ch. Merryhart Love Child, born November 1974, by Ch. Merryhart Honest John ex Ch. Merryhart Sound Off. Love Child belongs to Helen J. Love and Naomi Eberhardt.

THE WESTIE SHOW COAT

It is my opinion that no novice owner should ever attempt to prepare a Westie coat for the show ring without the help and instruction of someone knowledgeable in this regard. Competition within the breed has never been more keen than at present, and the manner in which your dog's coat has been prepared for his show career may well make the difference between a successful career and one which never gets off the ground.

One of the advantages of purchasing your Westie from a

from a book. To get the knack of doing up a dog that can hold its own against the professionals, you need the knowledge of a professional. So why not start out right in the first place?

Never have your show dog or show prospect groomed anywhere except at the kennel of a leading Westie breeder-exhibitor or a leading Westie handler who has the winning dogs

Ch. Dawn's Moment 'N' Time, by Ch. Biljonblues Best of Times ex Ch. Dawn's Vivacious Vivia 'N, C.G.C. Breeder-owners, Dawn L. Martin and Patrica H. Marks. His specialty wins include: 1991 WHWTC of Northern Ohio, Best in Sweeps; 1991 WHWTC of America, Montgomery County, Best of Opposite in Sweeps, Winners Dog, Best of Winners; 1992 WHWTC of S.E. Michigan, Winners Dog and Best of Winners.

to back up claims to knowledge. This success *must* include Westies, for the differences in coat care and presentation vary between breeds; and someone may be ever so great with one type terrier coat but not at all the same with our little white friends.

If you are intending to truly "go into" Westies as a lasting hobby or occupation, you owe it to yourself, and to the dogs who will share your future, to start out in the beginning with one of the leading handlers and learn everything you possibly can from that person. This will help equip you for taking it on later for yourself if you prefer; but observing the grooming, trimming, coat care, and showmanship of an expert at close range is definitely the way to go for someone who hopes to emulate this talent and the success it earns.

Winning Best in Sweepstakes and Reserve Winners Bitch at Associated Specialty Clubs of Indiana in 1989, **Dawn's Sweet 'N' Sassy,** by Am. and Can. Ch. Dawns Up 'N' Adam, Am. and Can. C.D.X. ex Sedora's McPersonable Ms. Bred by Judith A. Merritt. Owners, Eileen Barthold and Dawn L. Martin.

On Owning a West Highland White Terrier

The West Highland White Terrier is a very special dog, the ownership of which can bring a tremendous amount of pleasure to a dog-loving individual or to an entire family of canine enthusiasts. For here is a breed whose members fit right in with ease, seeming happy and at home in a very wide variety of situations.

First of all, before discussing his talents, let us take a look at the natural attributes of the breed. He is small, truly "handy home size"; but at the same time never could possibly be thought of as less than a very well-rounded, hardy personality who is ready for anything. He is definitely a family dog, devoted to all its members, from the senior citizens to the youngsters; and he seems to know instinctively how to get along amiably with anyone. He is a distinctive-looking fellow, tremendously eye-catching and appealing, a fact attested to by the number of artists who constantly choose him for posing for paintings, figurines, jewelry, etc., etc., all of which sell like hotcakes because Westies are so handsome, unique and endearing.

He is a perfect dog for any type of living. City dwellers find that his small size and good manners make him great for an apartment, where his short legs make the space adequate for him to keep in good health enjoying free run of the apartment,

Ch. Pagan Ghost, by Ch. Olac Mooncloud ex Purston Pagan Princess, is a famous Best in Show and Group-winning Westie belonging to Mr. and Mrs. George Seemann, Jr., Shelburne Kennels, South Norwalk, CT.

Nancy Spelke's first champion, known to his friends as "Westie P," more formally known as **Ch. Kilkerran Matinee Idol,** with a twinkle in his eye and a mouthful of cheese at home in Pasadena, CA.

dogs are noted, the Westie makes an alert, cheerful, inquisitive companion. A very "on the button" fellow who misses not a trick—for which reason he is also a superior watchdog, being quick to sound the alarm at the moment any strange or suspicious sound or person attracts his eye or ear. For any of you who doubt the effectiveness of a small dog as a household guardian, may I point out that often a little dog is quicker and more effective than a big one in announcing trouble or responding to suspicious circumstances; and while they are small, they are well equipped to excel in the area of barking up a storm, which is one of the chief hazards to be avoided in the opinions of persons up-to-no-good, anxious not to have their presence detected or announced.

Westies are very superior pets for children. Small, thus not likely to

supplemented by trips to the curb periodically and at least one walk of several blocks daily, which is beneficial for your health as well as for your Westie's.

Being a member of the terrier family, with all of the vitality and enjoyment of life for which these

Even great winning Westies have their favorite playthings, and here is "Kutter" with his. An informal pose of **Ch. Kilkerran 'N Wicket A Kut Above** at home in Pasadena, CA where he lives with his co-owner Nancy Spelke, whose expert presentation and conditioning have brought such great success to this excellent dog.

become overly rough during games with the kids, they are also reliable and truly do love kids, and are almost endlessly patient with them. This, I might add, does not mean that you should allow children to become overly rough in playing with the dog; nor to maul or hurt it and thus perhaps try the dog's patience and tolerance beyond endurance. Children should regard their pets as the live creatures they are rather than as toys, in which case they should receive considerate kindness rather than a test of their endurance—a fact which you should make clear to your own children and to any others who may also play with the puppy or dog. If there is a question, simply do not allow any children whom you feel are overly hard on a pet to fool with yours.

Terriers are mischievous—their eyes often seem to fairly sparkle with fun as they tease you for a bit of your time. They love your companionship, so taking a walk together, a game of ball, a trip in the car, or a run through the woods can be highly appreciated. By the same token, what counts most of all is the pleasure of being with you, so if you are in the mood for reading or watching television, or have desk work to do, your Westie will be equally happy to curl up along side of you, snoozing comfortably.

The Westie is an ideal dog for the suburbs or the country as well as for the more sedate city living. His terrier instincts are right there, making him glad to accept the task of keeping a farm rodent population well under control or whatever. However, one more frequently associates him with lending his handsome self to enhancing your home and property as a busy little household

Kilkerran foundation stock with breeders Kathy and Wayne Kompare. *Left to right,* **Ch. Kortni of Windy Hill, Ch. Jasmine of Windy Hill, Ch. Stonehedge Moonstone,** and **Flash Mac Tavish II.** Flash is the Kompare's first Westie.

family companion whose appearance seldom fails to bring an appreciative smile to the face of any but the most confirmed dog haters, for such an outgoing, responsive, intelligent, and all-around canine is mighty difficult to resist.

Being a terrier, the Westie is a very hardy breed demanding or needing very little in the way of coddling. They are good-doers with hearty appetites who thrive without an abundance of fuss.

Westies being terriers are in no way lacking courage, so if challenged by another dog will respond. Under ordinary circumstances, however, they get along well with one another and with your other pets too, but make certain that any individuals you plan to trust together do like one another.

Ch. Kortni of Windy Hill, by Ch. Loch Ness Mac Tavish, C.D. ex Ch. Glengarry Iveah of Windy Hill. Bred by Ann M. Frinks. Owned by Kathy and Wayne Kompare.

In all the hustle and crowd to be seen at Montgomery County, here is **Ch. Skaket's Candy Man, C.D.X., C.G., T.T.,** who is by Ch. Antic's of Abraxas ex Ch. Skaket's Lady MacDuff. This impressive homebred belongs to Nancy Gauthier and Mitzi Gauthier.

Your West Highland White Terrier and Obedience

For its own protection and safety, every dog should be taught, at the very least, to recognize and obey the commands "Come," "Heel," "Down," "Sit," and "Stay." Doing so at some time might save the dog's life and in less extreme circumstances will certainly make him a better behaved, more pleasant member of society. If you are patient and enjoy working with your dog, study some of the excellent books available on the subject of obedience and then teach your canine friend these basic manners. If you need the stimulus of working with a group, find out where obedience training classes are held (usually your veterinarian, your dog's breeder, or a dog-owning friend can tell you) and you and your dog can join. Alternatively, you could let someone else do the training by sending the dog to class, but this is not very rewarding because you lose the opportunity of working with your dog and the pleasure of the rapport thus established.

If you are going to do it yourself, there are some basic rules which you should follow. You must remain calm and confident in attitude. Never lose your temper and frighten or punish your dog unjustly. Be quick and lavish with praise each time a command is correctly followed. Make it fun for the dog and he will be eager to please you by responding correctly. Repetition is the keynote,

137

A legendary Westie from the past, one of the breed's immortals, this is **Ch. Purston Pinmoney Pedlar,** a 50-times Best in Show winner, who was owned by Mrs. B.G. Frame and handled throughout his fabulous show career by George Ward. Pictured taking Best in Specialty Show in Louisville in 1973.

quent teaching sessions should do the trick. If you have a problem working on your own, then you and the puppy should join a training class since working with others often goes better for both the trainer and the dog. You can, if you choose, even join a training class with the puppy, since some folks and some dogs find it easier working with a group than alone. Or, as a last resort, you can place the puppy in the hands of a professional trainer. But

but it should not be continued without recess to the point of tedium. Limit the training sessions to ten- or fifteen-minute periods at a time.

Westies are smart, sharp little people, thus they learn readily. A three-month-old puppy is not too young to begin simple obedience training for short periods of time once or twice daily. The key secrets to success are patience, repetition (although not carried on to the point of boredom for the puppy whose interest span is a short one), plus lots of rewards and praise when your commands are correctly obeyed. Never ever frighten the puppy or lose patience if he fails to understand as quickly as you feel he should. He is just a baby at that point, and patience plus short, fre-

in making this decision, do bear in mind the fact that in working with your puppy as you teach him you are establishing a wonderful rapport that will remain throughout the dog's lifetime. Do you not really feel this makes it worth the bit of extra time and effort involved in doing it yourself?

As you work with and train your baby Westie to be a well-behaved and responsible canine citizen as he grows, you also are doing the groundwork which might well open up a whole new field of enjoyment for you—obedience trials. Campaigning and working with your dog in competitive obedience trials as he earns titles are certain to bring you a proud feeling of accomplishment, and your dog too.

If you are enjoying teaching your dog the simple obedience basics and he seems to be learning with aptitude, why not take him to compete in an obedience match show or two, just to give it a "dry run." If all goes well, try next the Novice Class in obedience at your nearby dog show. (Go as a spectator a few times first in order to see how things are done.) You would be amazed how very many of our most successful exhibitors in the conformation competition, winners of multi-variety Groups and Best in Show, had their earliest dog show experiences with a puppy who started in obedience and learned to love the entire sport and thus became involved with it.

dog shows, with specialty shows, and frequently as separate specialty events. If you are working alone with your dog, a list of trial dates might be obtained from your dog's veterinarian, your dog breeder, or a dog-owning friend; the AKC *Gazette* lists shows and trials to be scheduled in the coming months; and if you are a member of a training class, you will find the information readily available.

Best in Show **Am. and Can. Ch. Dawn's Up 'N' Adam, Am. and Can. C.D.X., C.G.,** while working towards his obedience degrees in Canada. Bred and owned by Dawn L. Martin of Dawn's Highland Scots.

OBEDIENCE TRIALS

Formal obedience training can be followed, and very frequently is, by entering the dog in obedience competition to work toward an obedience degree, or several of them, depending on the dog's aptitude and your own enjoyment. Obedience trials are held in conjunction with the majority of all-breed conformation

The "Group Sit" obedience exercise here is demonstrated well by a group of Westies. Photo courtesy of Ralph Slater.

The goals for which one works in the formal AKC Member or Licensed Trials are the following titles: Companion Dog (C.D.), Companion Dog Excellent (C.D.X.), and Utility Dog (U.D.). These degrees are earned by receiving three "legs," or qualifying scores, at each level of competition. The degrees must be earned in order, with one completed prior to starting work on the next. For example, a dog must have earned C.D. prior to starting work on C.D.X.; then C.D.X. must be completed before U.D. work begins. The ultimate title attainable in obedience work is Obedience Trial Champion (O.T.Ch.)

When you see the letters C.D. following a dog's name, you will know that this dog has satisfactorily completed the following exercises: heel on leash and figure eight, heel free, stand for examination, recall, long sit, and long down. C.D.X. means that tests have been passed on all of those just mentioned plus heel free and figure eight, drop on recall, retrieve on flat, retrieve over high jump, broad jump, long sit, and long down. U.D. indicates that the dog has additionally passed tests in scent discrimination (leather article), scent discrimination (metal article), signal exercise, directed retrieve, directed jumping, and group stand for examination. The letters O.T.Ch. are the abbreviation for the only obedience title which precedes rather than follows a dog's name. To gain an obedience trial championship, a dog who already holds a Utility Dog degree must win a total of one hundred points and must win three firsts, under three different judges, in Utility and Open B Classes.

There is also a Tracking Dog title (T.D.) which can be earned at tracking trials. In order to pass the tracking tests the dog must follow the trail of a stranger along a path on which the trail was laid between thirty minutes and two hours previously. Along this track there must be more than two right-angle turns, at least two of which are well out in the open where no fences or other boundaries exist for the guidance of

A group of Westies obeying the "Down" command. Photo courtesy of Ralph Slater.

Ch. Skaket's Kit Kat, C.D.X., C.G., doing the "Seesaw" in Agility. Owned by Nancy and Mitzi Gauthier, Skaket Westies.

Ch. Skaket's Kit Kat, C.D.X., C.G., going down the "Dog Walk" in Agility. Nancy and Mitzi Gauthier owners.

Ch. Skatet's Kit Kat, C.D.X., C.G., climbing the "A" frame in Agility. Nancy and Mitzi Gauthier, owners.

The magnificent **Candy Man** doing the "Bar Jump" in Utility. Owned by Nancy and Mitzi Gauthier.

The Utility Class at the West Highland White Terrier Club of New England Fun Match. Courtesy of Nancy and Mitzi Gauthier. These Westies are doing a "Group Stand."

142

the dog or the handler. The dog wears a harness and is connected to the handler by a lead 20 to 40 feet in length. Inconspicuously dropped at the end of the track is an article to be retrieved, usually a glove or wallet, which the dog is expected to locate and the handler to pick up. The letters T.D.X. are the abbreviation for Tracking Dog Excellent, a more difficult version of the Tracking Dog test with a longer track and more turns to be worked through.

In the beginning there was little talk of Westies in obedience. To many they just did not seem quite suitable for that work. But in 1942, a little dog known as Champion Robinridge Bimelick was started on an obedience career by his owner, Mrs. Monroney, and the outcome was watched with interest and skepticism. But the skeptics had to eat their words: soon Champion Robinridge Bimelick, C.D., with the "X" denoting "Companion Dog Excellent" to be gained a few months later. Thus Bimelick, a show champion when he started on the road towards a C.D., was the first conformation champion Westie as well as the first of the breed to distinguish itself in obedience.

Bimelick remained Top Obedience Westie in the U.S. for a period of 16 years until 1958 when a Westie went still further up the ladder of obedience-competition success. This was a bitch named Katie McLeod, bred, owned and handled by Mrs. Margaret Barr, who earned for herself the title U.D. which

An 11-year-old **Ch. Skakat's Candy Man, U.D.T., C.G.,** with his flyball. Owned by Nancy and Mitzi Gauthier.

indicates earning a Utility Dog degree.

Nowadays it is old hat to observe the little Westies distinguishing themselves in this type competition as there have been lots more successes added to the lists. But at the period in time that Bimelick and Katie scored so well, both wins brought forth sincere congratulations, and we are certain gave impetus to those who have followed to take the step.

Ch. Skaket's Candy Man, U.D.T., C.G., in Utility at age 11 years. Owned by Nancy and Mitzi Gauthier.

The American Working Terrier Association (AWTA) has developed a test to determine the degree of hunting instinct in a terrier in a controlled setting and without the bloodshed which many people find objectionable. All across the United States, sanctioned trials are held nowadays which many Westie folk find fun and interesting. Even though one way of checking your dog's gameness is to take him out where there are rodents and see what he will do, many are reluctant to follow that procedure so opt for the AWTA trials.

The American Working Terrier Association accepts all A.K.C.-recognized terrier breeds of a size to fit into a nine-inch hole, plus Jack Russell Terriers and Glen of Imaal Terriers (neither are A.K.C. recognized) as well as Dachshunds to compete in these "going to ground" trials. The classification is divided into three categories: Novice "A" for inexperienced dogs of not more than one year's age; Novice "B" for inexperienced dogs a year's age or older; and an Open Class for dogs who have attained a score of 100 in Novice or are experienced hunters. From there a Certificate of Gameness can be earned, and the dog may be entered in the optional Certificate Class to compete for its breed's highest honors.

"Butch" spends a day visiting friends at the nursing home. Officially he is **Ch. Dawn's Son 'N' Heir,** a son of Best in Show Can. and Am. Ch. Dawn's Up 'N' Adam, Am. and Can. C.D.X., C.G., ex Scapa Flo. Butch was bred by Christine Bousquet and his owners are Nora Fabrycki and Dawn L. Martin.

For those of you who have never attended one of these AWTA events, here is how the "going to ground" exercise works. A nine-inch square wooden tunnel is buried in the ground, its entrance treated with the scent of game to emulate a real ground hole. At the end of the tunnel, live quarry is placed in a cage, which usually consists of several rats. The cage provides a barrier between the dogs and the quarry. The dog, waiting in the handler's arms eight feet away, has one minute exactly in which to spring into action when released, making his way towards the entrance. It is expected that he will exhibit high excitement upon entering the hole (going to ground) with lots of scratching and barking as he tries to reach the quarry. A trap door is provided through which the judge can watch what is taking place enabling each dog to be scored, and through which each can be lifted out at the completion of his turn to make way for the next one to follow. The quarry should be located and reached in a matter of seconds once the dog has been released to go find it, as the scent draws the terrier to the "ground" and he rushes inside. Scoring is in accordance with the speed of reaching the quarry

Ch. Skaket's Chunkies, U.D., C.G., performing in obedience class during 1976. Owners, Nancy Gauthier and Mitzi Gauthier.

Kay Sherrard putting her Westie through the obedience routine. Photo courtesy of Ralph Slater.

and the intensity of excitement generated, which should involve great scratching at the bars of the enclosure and much barking all to demonstrate true keenness and eagerness to get at the game.

The West Highland White Terrier Club of America has created a much esteemed honor to reward Westies who have accomplished any three of the following:

1.) Completion of an A.K.C. Championship.

2.) Earning an Obedience degree.

3.) Earning a Tracking degree.

4.) Earning a Working Certificate.

Needless to say, these awards, which are known as Versatility awards, are eagerly sought after and highly prized, as indeed they should be, by Westie owners who

145

enjoy helping to develop their wonderful breed's full potential.

The first recipient of a West Highland White Terrier Club of America Versatility award was Champion Skaket's Chunkies, U.D., C.G. In listing Chunkies's accomplishments, Nancy Gauthier notes: "First recipient of the Versatility award; five-point 'major,' Roving Specialty 1973; Five Group placements; Winner Stud Dog Classes, Montgomery 1975 and 1977; Stud Dog award; Utility degree; Certificate of Gameness; and climbed several mountains, including Mt. Washington."

Could anyone possibly hope for a more versatile and accomplished small canine? We think it would take quite a bit of "doing," especially when one adds to this a loving and devoted companion animal, the true happy, eager Westie personality, and success at just plain pleasing people, which Westies do so well.

An informal shot of **Ch. Kilkerran Matinee Idol** enjoying all the comforts of home. Nancy Spelke, owner, Pasadena, CA.

The Purchase of Your West Highland White Terrier

Careful consideration should be given to what breed of dog you wish to own prior to your purchase of one. If several breeds are attractive to you, and you are undecided as to which you prefer, learn all you can about the characteristics of each before making your decision. As you do so, you are thus preparing mains is to make a good choice.

It is never wise to just rush out and buy the first cute puppy who catches your eye. Whether you wish a dog to show, one with whom to compete in obedience, or one as a family dog purely for his (or her) companionship, the more time and thought you invest as you plan the

Kilkerran's "N" Litter at eight weeks old. By Ch. Whitebriar Jolliment ex Kilkerran Joy to the World. Kathy and Wayne Kompare, breeders-owners.

yourself to make an intelligent choice; and this is very important when buying a dog who will be, with reasonable luck, a member of your household for at least a dozen years or more. Obviously, since you are reading this book, you have decided on the breed—so now all that re- purchase, the more likely you are to meet with complete satisfaction. The background and early care behind your pet will reflect in the dog's future health and temperament. Even if you are planning the purchase purely as a pet, with no thoughts of showing or breeding in

147

Ch. Kilkerran Buccaneer, by Ch. London's Duffy Mac Duff ex Ch. Stonehedge Moonstone as a baby. Co-owned by breeders Kathy and Wayne Kompare, Kilkerran Westies, with Sue and Don Spicer.

the dog's or puppy's future, it is essential that, if the dog is to enjoy a trouble-free future, you assure yourself of a healthy, properly raised puppy or adult from sturdy, well-bred stock.

Throughout the pages of this book you will find the names and locations of many well-known and well-established kennels in various areas. Other sources of information are the American Kennel Club (51 Madison Avenue, New York, New York 10010) and the Kennel Club (1 Clarges Street, Piccadilly, London, W1Y 8AB) from whom you can obtain a list of recognized breeders in the vicinity of your home. If you plan to have your dog campaigned by a professional handler, by all means let the handler help you locate and select a good dog. Through their numerous clients, handlers have access to a variety of interesting show prospects; and the usual arrangement is that the handler resells the dog to you for what his cost has been, with the agreement that the dog be campaigned for you by him throughout the dog's career. It is most strongly recommended that prospective purchasers follow these suggestions, as you thus will be better able to locate and select a satisfactory puppy or dog.

Your first step in searching for your puppy is to make appointments at kennels specializing in your breed, where you can visit and inspect the dogs, both those available for sale and the kennel's basic breeding stock. You are looking for an active, sturdy puppy with bright eyes and intelligent expression and who is friendly and alert; avoid puppies who are hyperactive, dull, or listless. The coat should be clean and thick, with no sign of parasites. The premises on which he was raised should look (and smell) clean and be tidy, making it obvious that the puppies and their surroundings are in capable hands. Should the West Highland White kennels be sparse in your area or not have what you consider attractive, do not hesitate to contact others at a distance and purchase from them if they seem better able to supply a puppy or dog who will please you—*so long as it is a recognized breeding kennel of that breed.* Shipping dogs is a regular practice nowadays, with compara-tively few problems when one considers the number of dogs shipped each year. A reputable, well-known breeder wants the customer to be satisfied; thus, he will represent the puppy fairly. Should you not be pleased with the puppy upon arrival, a breeder, such as described, will almost certainly permit its return. A conscientious breeder takes real interest and concern in the welfare of the dogs he or she causes to be brought into the world. Such a breeder also is proud of a reputation for integrity. Thus on two counts, for the sake of the dog's future and the breeder's reputation, to such a person a *satisfied* customer takes precedence over a sale at any cost.

If your puppy is to be a pet or "family dog," the earlier the age at which it joins your household the better. Puppies are weaned and ready to start out on their own,

Just see all the promise for bright futures in these eight-week-old Westie babies. They became **Ch. Kilkerran The Joker is Wild** and **Kilkerran Joy to the World**. They were bred by Kathy and Wayne Kompare. Joker is co-owned by Brian Forrow.

under the care of a sensible new owner, at about six weeks old; and if you take a young one, it is often easier to train it to the routine of your household and to your requirements of it than is the case with an older dog which, even though still technically a puppy, may have already started habits you will find difficult to change. The younger puppy is usually less costly, too, as it stands to reason the breeder will not have as much expense invested in it. Obviously, a puppy that has been raised to five or six months old represents more in care and cash expenditure on the breeder's part than one sold earlier; therefore he should be, and generally is, priced accordingly.

There is an enormous amount of truth in the statement that "bargain" puppies seldom turn out to be that. A "cheap" puppy, raised purely for sale and profit, can and often does lead to great heartbreak, including problems and veterinarian's bills which can add up to many times the initial cost of a properly reared dog. On the other hand, just because a puppy is expensive does not assure one that is healthy and well reared. There have been numerous cases where unscrupulous dealers have sold, for several hundred dollars, puppies that were sickly, in poor condition, and such poor specimens that the breed of which they were supposedly members was barely recognizable. So one cannot always judge a puppy by price alone. Commonsense must guide a prospective purchaser, plus the selection of a *reliable*, well-recommended dealer whom you know to have well-satisfied customers or, best of all, a specialized breeder. You will probably find the fairest pricing at the kennel of a breeder. Such a person, experienced with the breed in general and with his or her own stock in particular, through extensive association with these dogs, has watched enough of them mature to have obviously learned to assess quite accurately each puppy's potential—something impossible where such background is non-existent.

One more word on the subject of pets. Bitches make a fine choice for this purpose as they are usually quieter and more gentle than the males, easier to house train, more affectionate, and less inclined to roam. If you do select a bitch and

A nine-week-old Westie puppy who grew up to be a top-quality winner. This one became **Ch. Raglan Ragtime Sophie Tucker** and proved a valuable asset to Penny-Belle Scorer's kennel.

Holyrood's Here Comes the Son, Holyrood's Ms. High Falutin, and **Holyrood's Karly With A "K",** littermates whose futures look bright at Shelly Bay Kennels.

have no intention of breeding or showing her, by all means have her spayed, for your sake and for hers. The advantages to the owner of a spayed bitch include avoiding the nuisance of "in season" periods which normally occur twice yearly—with the accompanying eager canine swains haunting your premises in an effort to get close to your female—plus the unavoidable messiness and spotting of furniture and rugs at this time, which can be annoying if she is a household companion in the habit of sharing your sofa or bed. As for the spayed bitch, she benefits as she grows older because this simple operation almost entirely eliminates the possibility of breast cancer ever occurring. It is recommended that all bitches eventually be spayed—even those used for show or breeding when their careers have ended—in order that they may enjoy a happier, healthier old age. Please take note, however, that a bitch who has been spayed (or an altered dog) *cannot be shown at American Kennel Club or Kennel Club dog shows once this operation has been performed.* Be certain that you are *not* interested in showing her before taking this step.

Also, in selecting a pet, never underestimate the advantages of an older dog, perhaps a retired show dog or a bitch no longer needed for breeding, who may be available and

A most promising eight-week-old puppy bitch who matured to become a famous winning bitch from Mrs. Johnston's Glenveagh Kennels, Ireland.

them and how to apply them to actual dogs before you are ready to make an intelligent selection of a show dog.

If you are thinking in terms of a dog to show, obviously you must have learned about dog shows and must be in the habit of attending them. This is fine, but now your activity in this direction should be increased, with your attending every single dog show within a reasonable distance from your home. Much can be learned about a breed at ringside at these events. Talk with the breeders who are exhibiting. Study the dogs they are showing. Watch the judging with concentration, noting each decision made, and attempt to follow the reasoning by which the judge has reached it. Note carefully the attributes of the dogs who win and, for your later use, the manner in which each is presented. Close your ears to the ringside know-it-alls, usually novice owners of a dog or two and very new to the Fancy, who have only derogatory remarks to make about all that is taking place unless they happen to win. This is the type of exhibitor who "comes and goes" through the Fancy and whose interest is usually of very short duration, owing to lack of knowledge and dissatisfaction caused by the failure to recognize the need to learn. You, as a fancier whom we hope will last and enjoy our sport over many future years, should develop independent thinking at this stage; you should learn to draw your own conclusions about the merits, or lack of them, seen before you in the ring

quite reasonably priced by a breeder anxious to place such a dog in a loving home. These dogs are settled and can be a delight to own, as they make wonderful companions, especially in a household of adults where raising a puppy can sometimes be a trial.

Everything that has been said about careful selection of your pet puppy and its place of purchase applies, but with many further considerations, when you plan to buy a show dog or foundation stock for a future breeding program. Now is the time for an in-depth study of the breed, starting with every word and every illustration in this book and all others you can find written on the subject. The Standard of the breed has now become your guide, and you must learn not only the words but also how to interpret and, thus, sharpen your own judgement in preparation for choosing wisely and well.

Note carefully which breeders campaign winning dogs—not just an occasional isolated good one, but consistent, homebred winners. It is from one of these people that you should select your own future "star."

If you are located in an area where dog shows take place only occasionally or where there are long travel distances involved, you will need to find another testing ground for your ability to select a worthy show dog. Possibly, there are some representative kennels raising this breed within a reasonable distance. If so, by all means ask permission of the owners to visit the kennels and do so when permission is granted. You may not necessarily buy then and there, as they may not have available what you are seeking that very day, but you will be able to see the type of dog being raised there and to discuss the dogs with the breeder. Every time you do this, you add to your knowledge. Should one of these kennels have dogs which especially appeal to you, perhaps you could reserve a show-prospect puppy from a coming litter. This is frequently done, and it is often worth waiting for a puppy, unless you have seen a dog with which you truly are greatly impressed and which is immediately available.

The purchase of a puppy has already been discussed. Obviously this same approach applies in a far greater degree when the purchase involved is a future show dog. The only place from which to purchase a show prospect is a breeder who raises show-type stock; otherwise,

Already training to become a show dog, this is **Ch. Holyrood's Hootman O' Shelly Bay** when just under four months old and still at home with his breeder, Marilyn Foster, Simsbury, CT. Manley was Top Westie in the U.S. and owned by Dr. James and Elizabeth Boso.

Ch. Wishing Well's Vister Colleen completing title at age eight months. Owner-handled by Barbara Worcester Keenan under noted judge, the late Winifred Heckmann.

you are almost certainly doomed to disappointment as the puppy matures. Show and breeding kennels obviously cannot keep all of their fine young stock. An active breeder-exhibitor is, therefore, happy to place promising youngsters in the hands of people also interested in showing and winning with them, doing so at a fair price according to the quality and prospects of the dog involved. Here again, if no kennel in your immediate area has what you are seeking, do not hesitate to contact top breeders in other areas and to buy at long distance. Ask for pictures, pedigrees, and a complete description. Heed the breeder's advice and recommendations, after truthfully telling exactly what your expectations are for the dog you purchase. Do you want something with which to win just a few ribbons now and then? Do you want a dog who can complete his championship? Are you thinking of the real "big time" (i.e., seriously campaigning with Best of Breed,

Kilkerran Moonstruck, by Ch. Whitebriar Jollimont ex Ch. Holyrood's Liza with a "Z", was co-bred by Judy Francisco with owners Kathy and Wayne Kompare.

Group wins, and possibly even Best in Show as your eventual goal)? Consider it all carefully in advance; then honestly discuss your plans with the breeder. You will be better satisfied with the results if you do this, as the breeder is then in the best position to help you choose the dog who is most likely to come through for you. A breeder selling a show dog is just as anxious as the buyer for the dog to succeed, and the breeder will represent the dog to you with truth and honesty. Also, this type of breeder does not lose interest the moment the sale has been made but, when necessary, will be right there to assist you with beneficial advice and suggestions based on years of experience.

Kilkerran Joy to the World and **Ch. Kilkerran The Joker is Wild,** co-owned by Brian Forrow—both puppies are age eight weeks. Breeders-co-owners, Kathy and Wayne Kompare, Kilkerran, Danbury, CT.

As you make inquiries of at least several kennels, keep in mind that show-prospect puppies are less expensive than mature show dogs, the latter often costing close to four figures, and sometimes more. The reason for this is that, with a puppy, there is always an element of chance, the possibility of its developing unexpected faults as it matures or failing to develop the excellence and quality that earlier had seemed probable. There definitely is a risk factor in buying a show-prospect puppy. Sometimes all goes well, but occasionally the swan becomes an ugly duckling. Reflect on this as you consider available puppies and young adults. It just might be a good idea to go with a more mature, though more costly, dog if one you like is available.

When you buy a mature show dog, "what you see is what you get," and it is not likely to change beyond coat and condition, which are dependent on your care. Also advantageous for a novice owner is the fact that a mature dog of show quality almost certainly will have received show-ring training and probably match-show experience, which will make your earliest handling ventures much easier.

Frequently it is possible to purchase a beautiful dog who has completed championship but who, owing to similarity in bloodlines, is not

A future Best in Show winner while still a youngster winning the first of three specialty placements from the Bred-by-Exhibitor Class, including the National Specialty in 1983. The Kompares' **Ch. Kilkerran D'Artagnon** judged by Westie expert Barbara Keenan.

needed for the breeder's future program. Here you have the opportunity of owning a champion, usually in the two-to-five-year-old range, which you can enjoy campaigning as a special (for Best of Breed competition) and which will be a settled, handsome dog for you and your family to enjoy with pride.

If you are planning foundation for a future kennel, concentrate on acquiring one or two really superior bitches. These need not be top show-quality, but they should represent your breed's finest producing bloodlines from a strain noted for producing quality, generation after genera-

tion. A proven matron who is already the dam of show-type puppies is, of course, the ideal selection; but these are usually difficult to obtain, no one being anxious to part with so valuable an asset. You just might strike it lucky, though, in which case you are off to a flying start. If you cannot find such a matron available, select a young bitch of finest background from top-producing lines who is herself of decent type, free of obvious faults, and of good quality.

Great attention should be paid to the pedigree of the bitch from whom you intend to breed. If not already known to you, try to see the sire and dam. It is generally agreed that someone starting with a breed should concentrate on a fine collection of topflight bitches and raise a few litters from these before considering keeping one's own stud dog. The practice of buying a stud and then breeding everything you own or acquire to that dog does not always work out well. It is better to take advantage of the many noted sires who are available to be used at stud, who represent all of the leading strains, and, in each case, to carefully select the one who in type and pedigree seems most compatible to

each of your bitches, at least for your first several litters.

To summarize, if you want a "family dog" as a companion, it is best to buy it young and raise it according to the habits of your household. If you are buying a show dog, the more mature it is, the more certain you can be of its future beauty. If you are buying foundation stock for a kennel, then bitches are better, but they must be from the finest *producing* bloodlines.

When you buy a pure-bred dog that you are told is eligible for registration, you are entitled to receive from the seller an application form

Owned by Eileen Barthold and Dawn L. Martin, **Dawn's Sweet "N" Sassy** was bred by Judith A. Merritt, and was sired by Am. and Can. Ch. Dawn's Up 'N' Adam, Am. and Can. C.D.X., C.G. ex Sedora's Mc Personable Ms. Pictured here as a youngster during 1989 winning a splendid Best in Sweepstakes at the Associated Specialty Clubs of Indiana.

which will enable you to register your dog. If the seller cannot give you the application form, you should demand and receive an identification of your dog, consisting of the name of the breed, the registered names and numbers of the sire and dam, the name of the breeder, and your dog's date of birth. If the litter of which your dog is a part is already recorded with the registry Club, then the litter number is sufficient identification.

Do not be misled by promises of papers at some later date. Demand a registration application form or proper identification as described above. If neither is supplied, do not buy the dog. Proper paper work is especially important in the purchase of show or breeding stock.

Former professional handler now turned judge, Mrs. Dora Lee Wilson with Eve Varley's **Ch. Riversides Jolly Imp,** one of the many Westie "stars" she handled so outstandingly. This photo was taken shortly before Mrs. Wilson's retirement from handling.

158

The Care of Your West Highland White Terrier Puppy

The moment you decide to be the new owner of a puppy is not one second too soon to start planning for the puppy's arrival in your home. Both the new family member and you will find the transition period easier if your home is geared in advance of the arrival.

The first things to be prepared are a bed for the puppy and a place where you can pen him up for rest periods. Every dog should have a crate of its own from the very beginning, so that he will come to know and love it as his special place where he is safe and happy. It is an ideal arrangement, for when you want him to be free, the crate stays open. At other times you can securely latch it and know that the pup is safely out of mischief. If you travel with him, his crate comes along in the car; and, of course, in traveling by plane there is no alternative but to have a carrier for the dog. If you show your dog, you will want him upon occasion to be in a crate a good deal of the day. So from every consideration, a crate is a very sensible and sound investment in your puppy's future safety and happiness and for your own peace of mind.

The crates most desirable are the wooden ones with removable side panels, which are ideal for cold weather (with the panels in place to keep out drafts) and in hot weather (with the panels removed to allow better air circulation). Wire crates are all right in the summer, but they give no protection from cold or drafts. Aluminum crates, due to the manner in which the metal re-

Four-month-old puppies at Mrs. M. Johnston's kennel in Ireland. These are **Glenveagh Gabriella** and **Glenveagh Lady Arabella**.

flects surrounding temperatures, are not recommended. If it is cold, so is the metal of the crate; if it is hot, the crate becomes burning hot.

When you choose the puppy's crate, be certain that it is roomy enough not to become outgrown. The crate should have sufficient height so the dog can stand up in it as a mature dog and sufficient area

159

so that he can stretch out full length when relaxed. When the puppy is young, first give him shredded newspaper as a bed; the papers can be replaced with a mat or turkish towels when the dog is older. Carpet remnants are great for the bottom of the crate, as they are inexpensive and in case of accidents can be quite easily replaced. As the dog matures and is past the chewing

Westie puppies in the woods. Owned by Dale L. McDonald, Sutherlin, OR.

age, a pillow or blanket in the crate is an appreciated comfort.

Sharing importance with the crate is a safe area in which the puppy can exercise and play. If you are an apartment dweller, a baby's playpen works out well for a young dog; for an older puppy use a portable exercise pen which you can use later when travelling with your dog or for dog shows. If you have a yard, an area where he can be outside in safety should be fenced in prior to the dog's arrival at your home. This area does not need to be huge, but it does need to be made safe and secure. If you are in a suburban area where there are close neighbors, stockade fencing works out best, as then the neighbors are less aware of the dog and the dog cannot see and bark at everything passing by. If you are out in the country where no problems with neighbors are likely to occur, then regular chain-link fencing is fine. For added precaution in both cases, use a row of concrete blocks or railroad ties inside against the entire bottom of the fence; this precludes or at least considerably lessens the chances of your dog digging his way out.

Be advised that if yours is a single dog, it is very unlikely that it will get sufficient exercise just sitting in the fenced area, which is what most of them do when they are there alone. Two or more dogs will play and move themselves around, but one by itself does little more than make a leisurely tour once around the area to check things over and then lie down. You must include a daily walk or two in your plans if your puppy is to be rugged and well. Exercise is extremely important to a puppy's muscular development and to keep a mature dog fit and trim. So make sure that those exercise periods, or walks, a game of ball, and other such activities, are part of your daily program as a dog owner.

If your fenced area has an outside gate, provide a padlock and key and a strong fastening for it, and use

Marilyn Foster owns this handsome young Westie, **Holyrood's Here Comes The Son,** for whom a very bright future is anticipated. By Ch. Glenfinnan Something Dandy ex Ch. Holyrood's Liza with a "Z", he is campaigned by Jay Richardson and is already a proven sire of outstanding quality.

them, so that the gate cannot be opened by others and the dog taken or turned free. The ultimate convenience in this regard is, of course, a door (unused for other purposes) from the house around which the fenced area can be enclosed, so that all you have to do is open the door and out into his area he goes. This arrangement is safest of all, as then you need not be using a gate, and it is easier in bad weather since then you can send the dog out without taking him and becoming soaked yourself at the same time. This is not always possible to manage, but if your house is arranged so that you could do it this way, you would never regret it due to the convenience and added safety thus provided. Fencing in the entire yard, with gates to be opened and closed whenever a caller, deliveryman, postman, or some other person comes on your property, really is not safe at all because people not used to gates are frequently careless about closing and latching them *securely.* Many heartbreaking incidents have been brought about by someone carelessly half closing a gate (which the owner had thought to be firmly latched) and the dog wandering out. For greatest security a fenced *area* definitely takes precedence over a fenced *yard.*

The puppy will need a collar (one that fits now, not one to be grown into) and a lead from the moment you bring him home. Both should be an appropriate weight and type for his size. Also needed are a feeding dish and a water dish, both made preferably of unbreakable material. Your pet supply shop should have an interesting assortment of these and other accessories from which you can choose. Then you will need grooming tools of the type the breeder recommends and some toys. Equally satisfactory is Nylabone®, a nylon bone that does not chip or splinter and that "frizzles" as the puppy chews, providing healthful gum massage. Avoid plastics and any sort of rubber toys, *particularly those with squeakers* which the puppy may remove and swallow. If you want a ball for the puppy to use when playing with him, select one of very hard construction made for this purpose and do not leave it alone with him because he may chew off and swallow bits of the rubber. Take the ball with you when the game is over. This also applies to some of those "tug of war" type rubber toys which are fun when used with the two of you for that purpose but again should *not* be left behind for the dog to work on with his teeth. Bits of swallowed rubber, squeakers, and other such foreign articles can wreak great havoc in the intestinal tract— do all you can to guard against them.

Too many changes all at once can be difficult for a puppy. For at least the first few days he is with you, keep him on the food and feeding schedule to which he is accus- tomed. Find out ahead of time from the breeder what he feeds his puppies, how frequently, and at what times of the day. Also find out what, if any, food supplements the breeder has been using and recommends. Then be prepared by getting in a supply of the same food so that you will have it there when you bring the puppy home. Once the puppy is accustomed to his new surroundings, then you can switch the type of food and schedule to fit your convenience, but for the first several days do it as the puppy expects.

Your selection of a veterinarian should also be attended to before the puppy comes home, because you should stop at the vet's office for the puppy to be checked over as soon as you leave the breeder's premises. If the breeder is from your area, ask him for recommendations. Ask your dog-owning friends for their opinions of the local veterinarians,

Duffy and **Punch** on the hunt. Gale L. McDonald, owner.

Raglan Westies at home on the lawn. All proudly owned by Raglan Kennels, Penny-Belle Scorer, Richmond Hill, Ontario, Canada.

and see what their experiences with those available have been. Choose someone whom several of your friends recommend highly, then contact him about your puppy, perhaps making an appointment to stop in at his office. If the premises are clean, modern, and well equipped, and if you like the veterinarian, make an appointment to bring the puppy in on the day of purchase. Be sure to obtain the puppy's health record from the breeder, including information on such things as shots and worming that the puppy has had.

JOINING THE FAMILY

Remember that, exciting and happy an occasion as it is for you, the puppy's move from his place of birth to your home can be, for him, a traumatic experience. His mother and littermates will be missed. He quite likely will be awed or frightened by the change of surroundings. The person on whom he depended will be gone. Everything should be planned to make his arrival at your home pleasant—to give him confidence and to help him realize that yours is a pretty nice place to be after all.

Never bring a puppy home on a holiday. There is just too much going on with people and gifts and excitement. If he is in honor of an "occasion," work it out so that his arrival will be a few days earlier, or perhaps even better, a few days later than the "occasion." Then your home will be back to its normal routine and the puppy can enjoy your undivided attention. Try not to bring the puppy home in the evening. Early morning is the ideal time, as then he has the opportunity of getting acquainted and the

163

initial strangeness should wear off before bedtime. You will find it a more peaceful night that way. Allow the puppy to investigate as he likes, under your watchful eye. If you already have a pet in the household, keep a careful watch that the relationship between the two gets off to a friendly start or you may quickly find yourself with a lasting problem. Much of the future attitude of each toward the other will depend on what takes place that first day, so keep your mind on what they are doing and let your other activities slide for the moment. Be careful not to let your older pet become jealous by paying more attention to the puppy than to him, as that will start a bad situation immediately.

Westies are natural clowns—**"Stuart"** on Halloween dressed for the festivities. Penny-Belle Scorer owner.

If you have a child, here again it is important that the relationship start out well. Before the puppy is brought home, you should have a talk with the youngster. He must clearly understand that puppies are fragile and can easily be injured; therefore, they should not be teased, hurt, mauled, or overly rough-housed. A puppy is not an inanimate toy; it is a living thing with a right to be loved and handled respectfully, treatment which will reflect in the dog's attitude toward your child as both mature together. Never permit your children's playmates to mishandle the puppy, tormenting the puppy until it turns on the children in self-defense. Children often do not realize how rough is too rough. You, as a responsible adult, are obligated to assure that your puppy's relationship with children is a pleasant one.

Do not start out by spoiling your puppy. A puppy is usually pretty smart and can be quite demanding. What you had considered to be "just for tonight" may be accepted by the puppy as "for keeps." Be firm with him, strike a routine, and stick to it. The puppy will learn more quickly this way, and everyone will be happier as a result. A radio playing softly or a dim night light are often comforting to a puppy as it gets accustomed to new surroundings and should be provided in preference to bringing the puppy to bed with you—unless, of course, you intend him to share the bed as a permanent arrangement.

SOCIALIZING AND TRAINING

Socialization and training of your puppy should start the very day of his arrival in your home. Never address him without calling him by name. A short, simple name is the easiest to teach as it catches the dog's attention quickly; avoid elaborate call names. Always address the dog by the same name, not a whole series of pet names; the latter will only confuse the puppy.

Use his name clearly, and call the puppy over to you when you see him awake and wandering about. When he comes, make a big fuss over him for being such a good dog. He thus will quickly associate the sound of his name with coming to you and a pleasant happening.

Several hours after the puppy's arrival is not too soon to start accustoming him to the feel of a light collar. He may hardly notice it; or he may struggle, roll over, and try to rub it off his neck with his paws. Divert his attention when this occurs by offering a tasty snack or a toy (starting a game with him) or by petting him. Before long he will have accepted the strange feeling around his neck and no longer appear aware

Good action in a Westie Puppy illustrated by **Manley**. Photo courtesy of Marilyn Foster.

of it. Next comes the lead. Attach it and then immediately take the puppy outside or otherwise try to divert his attention with things to see and sniff. He may struggle against the lead at first, biting at it and trying to free himself. Do not pull him with it at this point; just hold the end loosely and try to follow him if he starts off in any direction. Normally his attention will soon turn to investigating his surroundings if he is outside or you have taken him into an unfamiliar room in your house; curiosity will take over and he will become interested in sniffing around the surroundings. Follow him with the lead slackly held until he seems to have completely forgotten about it; then try with gentle

165

urging to get him to follow you. Don't be rough or jerk at him; just tug gently on the lead in short quick motions (steady pulling can become a battle of wills), repeating his name or trying to get him to follow your hand which is holding a bit of food or an interesting toy. If you have an older lead-trained dog, then it should be a cinch to get the puppy to follow along after *him*. In any event the average puppy learns quite quickly and will soon be trotting along nicely on the lead. Once that point has been reached, the next step is to teach him to follow on your left side, or heel. This will not likely be accomplished all in one day; it should be done with short training periods over the course of several days until you are satisfied with the result.

During the course of house training your puppy, you will need to take him out frequently and at regular intervals: first thing in the morning directly from the crate, immediately after meals, after the puppy has been napping, or when you notice that the puppy is looking for a spot. Choose more or less the same place to take the puppy each time so that a pattern will be established. If he does not go immediately, do not return him to the house as he will probably relieve himself the moment he is inside. Stay out with him until he has finished; then be lavish with your praise for his good behavior. If you catch the puppy having an accident indoors, grab him firmly and rush him outside, sharply saying "No!" as you pick him up. If you do not see the accident occur, there is little point in doing anything except cleaning it up, as once it has happened and been forgotten, the puppy will most likely not even realize why you are scolding him.

If you live in a big city or are away many hours at a time, having a dog that is trained to go on paper has some very

Westies love playing in the snow, as illustrated by this happy group from Penny-Belle Scorer's Canadian Raglan Kennels in Richmond Hill, Ontario. They are indeed very handsome Westies!

definite advantages. To do this, one proceeds pretty much the same way as taking the puppy outdoors, except now you place the puppy on the newspaper at the proper time. The paper should always be kept in the same spot. An easy way to paper train a puppy if you have a playpen for it or an exercise pen is to line the area with newspapers; then gradually, every day or so, remove a section of newspaper until you are down

Handler Chris Steele with **Am. and Can. Glengidge Happy Hooligan,** owned by Mark and Judy Lewis, Neptune, NJ.

to just one or two. The puppy acquires the habit of using the paper; and as the prepared area grows smaller, in the majority of cases the dog will continue to use whatever paper is still available. It is pleasant, if the dog is alone for an excessive length of time, to be able to feel that if he needs it the paper is there and will be used.

The puppy should form the habit of spending a certain amount of time in his crate, even when you are home. Sometimes the puppy will do this voluntarily, but if not, he should be taught to do so, which is accomplished by leading the puppy over by his collar, gently pushing him inside, and saying firmly, "Down" or "Stay." Whatever expression you use to give a command, stick to the very same one each time for each act. Repetition is the big thing in training—and so is association with what the dog is expected to do. When you mean "Sit," always say exactly that. "Stay" should mean *only* that the dog should remain where he receives the command. "Down" means something else again. Do not confuse the dog by shuffling the commands, as this will create training problems for you.

As soon as he has had his immunization shots, take your puppy with you whenever and wherever possible. There is nothing that will

Glengidge Golden Charm, by Ch. Dalriada's Sam I Am ex Glengidge Golden Girl, C.D., is owned by Helene and Seymour Weiss and was bred by Winnie Kelly. Here she is receiving the award for Best Puppy in Show at the Terrier Breeders Association of Canada 1990 event from judge Donald F. White. This youngster was 11 months old at the time and was owner-handled by Helene Weiss to this very coveted victory.

build a self-confident, stable dog like socialization, and it is extremely important that you plan and give the time and energy necessary for this, whether your dog is to be a show dog or a pleasant, well-adjusted family member. Take your puppy in the car so that he will learn to enjoy riding and not become carsick, as dogs may do if they are infrequent travelers. Take him anywhere you are going where you are certain he will be welcome: visiting friends and relatives (if they do not have housepets who may resent the visit), busy shopping centers (keeping him always on lead), or just walking around the streets of your town. If someone admires him (as always seems to happen when one is out with puppies), encourage the stranger to pet and talk with him.

THE CARE OF YOUR WEST HIGHLAND WHITE TERRIER PUPPY

Socialization of this type brings out the best in your puppy and helps him to grow up with a friendly outlook, liking the world and its inhabitants. The worst thing that can be done to a puppy's personality is to shelter him. By always keeping him at home away from things and people unfamiliar to him, you may be creating a personality problem for the mature dog that will be a cross for you to bear later on.

Am. and Can. Ch. Sno-Bilt's Eliminator, owned by Shane Albee, Pearland, TX, is a noted specialty and Group winner plus a sire of distinction with famous winners to his credit. Handled by Chris Steele, he is pictured winning Best of Breed at Longshore-Southport in June 1989.

Am. and Ber. Ch. Sno-Bilt's Brag Time, by Happy Mac's An' Tigger Too ex Sno-Bilt's Sagitta. Bred by Gwyn Ellis and Jodine Vertuno; owned by Mrs. Vertuno.

Breeding Your West Highland White Terrier

The first responsibility of any person breeding dogs is to do so with care, forethought, and deliberation. It is inexcusable to breed more litters than you need to carry on your show program or to perpetuate your bloodlines. A responsible breeder should not cause a litter to be born without definite plans for the safe and happy disposition of the puppies.

A responsible dog breeder makes absolutely certain, so far as is humanly possible, that the home to which one of his puppies will go is a good home, one that offers proper care and an enthusiastic owner. To be admired are those breeders who insist on visiting (although doing so is not always feasible) the prospective owners of their puppies to see if they have suitable facilities for keeping a dog, to find out if they understand the responsibility involved, and to make certain if all members of the household are in accord regarding the desirability of owning one. All breeders should carefully check out the credentials of prospective purchasers to be sure that the puppy is being placed in responsible hands.

No breeder ever wants a puppy or grown dog he has raised to wind up in an animal shelter, in an experimental laboratory, or as a victim of a speeding car. While complete control of such a situation may be impossible, it is important to make every effort to turn over dogs to responsible people. When selling a puppy, it is a good idea to do so with the understanding that should it become necessary to place the dog in other hands, the purchaser will first contact you, the breeder. You may want to help in some way, possibly by buying or taking back the dog or placing it elsewhere. It is not fair to sell puppies and then never again give a thought to their welfare. Family problems arise, people may be forced to move where dogs are prohibited, or people just

Two of the Cloudcroft Westies, owned by the McDonalds, Sutherlin, OR.

171

grow bored with a dog and its care. Thus the dog becomes a victim. You, as the dog's breeder, should concern yourself with the welfare of each of your dogs and see to it that the dog remains in good hands.

The final obligation every dog owner shares, be there just one dog or an entire kennel involved, is that of making detailed, explicit plans for the future of these dearly loved animals in the event of the owner's death. Far too many people are apt to procrastinate and leave this very important matter unattended to, feeling that everything will work out or that "someone will see to them." Neither is too likely, at least not to the benefit of the dogs, unless you have done some advance planning which will assure their future well-being.

Life is filled with the unexpected, and even the youngest, healthiest, most robust of us may be the victim of a fatal accident or sudden illness. The fate of your dogs, so entirely in your hands, should never be left to chance. If you have not already done so, please get together with your lawyer and set up a clause in your will specifying what you want done with each of your dogs, to whom they will be entrusted (after first making absolutely certain that the person selected is willing and able to assume the responsibility), and telling the locations of all registration papers, pedigrees, and kennel records. Just think of the possibilities which might happen otherwise! If there is another family member who shares your love of the dogs, that is good and you have less to worry about. But if your heirs are not dog-oriented, they will hardly know how to proceed or how to cope with the dogs themselves, and they may wind up disposing of or caring for your dogs in a manner that would break your heart were you around to know about it.

It is advisable to have in your will specific instructions concerning each of your dogs. A friend, also a dog person who regards his or her own dogs with the same concern and

Punch with her babies at Cloudcroft Westies in the privacy of her whelping box. Gale C. McDonald owner.

We love this photo from Marilyn Foster, of **Ch. Holyrood's Hotspur O'Shelly Bay** (Ted) and **Holyrood's Wildbill O'Shelly Bay** (Bill), littermates born January 28, 1990. These two napping youngsters are half-brothers to Ch. Holyrood's Hootnanny O'Shelly Bay from the same dam, Holyrood's Mayhem (Shelby), and sired by Holyrood's Here Comes The Son.

esteem as you do, may agree to take over their care until they can be placed accordingly and will make certain that all will work out as you have planned. This person's name and phone number can be prominently displayed in your van or car and in your wallet. Your lawyer can be made aware of this fact. This can be spelled out in your will. The friend can have a signed check of yours to be used in case of an emergency or accident when you are traveling with the dogs; this check can be used to cover his or her expense to come and take over the care of your dogs should anything happen to make it impossible for you to do so. This is the least any dog owner should do in preparation for the time their dogs suddenly find themselves alone. There have been so many sad cases of dogs unprovided for by their loving owners, left to heirs who couldn't care less and who disposed of them in any way at all to get rid of them, or left to heirs who kept and neglected them under the misguided idea that they were providing them "a fine home with lots of freedom." These misfortunes must be prevented from befalling your own dogs who have meant so much to you!

Conscientious breeders feel quite strongly that the only possible reason for producing puppies is the ambition to improve and uphold quality and temperament within the breed—definitely *not* because one hopes to make a quick cash profit on a mediocre litter, which never seems to work out that way in the long run and which accomplishes little beyond perhaps adding to the nation's heartbreaking number of unwanted canines. The only reason ever for breeding a litter is, with conscientious people, a desire to improve the quality of dogs in their own kennel or, as pet owners, to add to the number of dogs they themselves own with a puppy or two from their present favorites. In either case, breeding should not take place unless one definitely has prospective owners for as many puppies as the litter may contain, lest you find yourself with several fast-growing young dogs and no homes in which to place them.

THE BROOD BITCH

Bitches should not be mated earlier than their second season, by which time they should be from fifteen to eighteen months old. Many breeders prefer to wait and finish the championships of their show bitches before breeding them, as pregnancy can be a disaster to a show coat and getting the bitch back in shape again takes time. When you have decided what will be the proper time, start watching at least several months ahead for what you feel would be the perfect mate to best complement your bitch's quality and bloodlines. Subscribe to the magazines which feature your breed exclusively and to some which cover all breeds in order to familiarize yourself with outstanding stud dogs in areas other than your own, for there is no necessity nowadays to limit your choice to a local dog unless you truly like him and feel that he is the most suitable. It is quite

usual to ship a bitch to a stud dog a distance away, and this generally works out with no ill effects. The important thing is that you need a stud dog strong in those features where your bitch is weak, a dog whose bloodlines are compatible with hers. Compare the background

Yes, you're counting correctly—there are nine two-day-old Westie babies in this picture with their dam. They belong to D. and D. Kennels in Idaho, owned by Dick and Dee Hanna.

of both your bitch and the stud dog under consideration, paying particular attention to the quality of the puppies from bitches with backgrounds similar to your bitch's. If the puppies have been of the type and quality you admire, then this dog would seem a sensible choice for yours, too.

Stud fees may be a few hundred dollars, sometimes even more under special situations for a particularly successful sire. It is money well spent, however. *Do not* ever breed to a dog because he is less expensive than the others unless you honestly believe that he can sire the kind of puppies who will be a credit to your kennel and your breed.

Contacting the owners of the stud dogs you find interesting will bring you pedigrees and pictures which you can then study in relation to your bitch's pedigree and conformation. Discuss your plans with other breeders who are knowledgeable (including the one who bred your own bitch). You may not always receive an entirely unbiased opinion (particularly if the person giving it also has an available stud dog), but one learns by discussion so listen to what they say, consider their opinions, and then you may be better qualified to form your own opinion.

As soon as you have made a choice, phone the owner of the stud dog you wish to use to find out if this will be agreeable. You will be asked about the bitch's health, soundness, temperament, and freedom from serious faults. A copy of her pedigree may be requested, as might a picture of her. A discussion of her background over the telephone may be sufficient to assure the stud's owner that she is suitable for the stud dog and that she is of type, breeding, and quality herself, capable of producing the kind

of puppies for which the stud is noted. The owner of a top-quality stud is often extremely selective in the bitches permitted to be bred to his dog, in an effort to keep the standard of his puppies high. The owner of a stud dog may require that the bitch be tested for brucellosis, which should be attended to not more than a month previous to the breeding.

Check out which airport will be most convenient for the person meeting and returning the bitch, if she is to be shipped, and also what airlines use that airport. You will find that the airlines are also apt to have special requirements concerning acceptance of animals for shipping. These include weather limitations and types of crates which are acceptable. The weather limits have to do with extreme heat and extreme cold at the point of destination, as some airlines will not fly

Westie puppies resting up after a busy day. They are **Ready** and **Manley,** owned by Marilyn Foster, Shelly Bay West Highlands, Simsbury, CT.

Ch. Holyrood's Ms. Mayhem, a dam who has contributed greatly to quality in the Westie breed. Owned by Marilyn Foster at Shelly Bay.

be careful to avoid shipping her on a weekend when schedules often vary and freight offices are apt to be closed. Whenever you can, ship your bitch on a direct flight. Changing planes always carries a certain amount of risk of a dog being overlooked or wrongly routed at the middle stop, so avoid this danger if at all possible. The bitch must be accompanied by a health certificate which you must obtain from your veterinarian before taking her to the airport. Usually it will be necessary to have the bitch at the airport about two hours prior to flight time. Before finalizing arrangements, find out from the stud's owner at what time of day it will be most convenient to have the bitch picked up promptly upon arrival.

It is simpler if you can bring the bitch to the stud dog yourself. Some people feel that the trauma of the flight may cause the bitch to not conceive; and, of course, undeniably there is a slight risk in shipping which can be avoided if you are able to drive the bitch to her destination. Be sure to leave yourself sufficient time to assure your arrival at the

dogs into temperatures above or below certain levels, fearing for their safety. The crate problem is a simple one, since, if your own crate is not suitable, most of the airlines have specially designed crates available for purchase at a fair and moderate price. It is a good plan to purchase one of these if you intend to be shipping dogs with any sort of frequency. They are made of fiberglass and are the safest type to use for shipping.

Normally you must notify the airline several days in advance to make a reservation, as they are able to accommodate only a certain number of dogs on each flight. Plan on shipping the bitch on about her eighth or ninth day of season, but right time for her for breeding (normally the tenth to fourteenth day following the first signs of color); and remember that if you want the bitch bred twice, you should allow a day to elapse between the two matings. Do not expect the stud's owner to house you while you are there. Locate a nearby motel that takes dogs and make that your headquarters.

Just prior to the time your bitch is due in season, you should take her to visit your veterinarian. She should be checked for worms and should receive all the booster shots for which she is due plus one for parvovirus, unless she has had the latter shot fairly recently. The brucellosis test can also be done then, and the health certificate can be obtained for shipping if she is to travel by air. Should the bitch be at all overweight, now is the time to get the surplus off. She should be in good condition, neither underweight nor overweight, at the time of breeding.

The moment you notice the swelling of the vulva, for which you should be checking daily as the time for her season approaches, and the appearance of color, immediately contact the stud's owner and settle on the day for shipping or make the appointment for your arrival with the bitch for breeding. If you are shipping the bitch, the stud fee check should be mailed immediately, leaving ample time for it to have been received when the bitch arrives and the mating takes place. Be sure to call the airline, making her reservation at that time, too.

Do not feed the bitch within a few hours before shipping her. Be certain that she has had a drink of water and been well exercised before closing her in the crate. Several layers of newspapers, topped with some shredded newspaper, make a good bed and can be discarded when she arrives at her destination; these can be replaced with fresh newspapers for her return home. Remember that the bitch should be brought to the airport about two hours before flight time, as sometimes the airlines refuse to accept late arrivals.

Enjoying just sitting around at home, **Ch. Kilkerran Matinee Idol** was bred by the Kompares and is owned by Nancy Spelke, Pasadena, CA.

A homebred sire of 85 champions, **Ch. Mac-Ken-Char's Irish Navigator** is winning Best in Specialty Show at the Western Reserve K.C. under breeder-judge Seymour Weiss *(center left)*. This was Navigator's second victory at this important show. Co-owned by Joanne Glodek and Jaimi Glodek.

If you are taking your bitch by car, be certain that you will arrive at a reasonable time of day. Do not appear late in the evening. If your arrival in town is not until late, get a good night's sleep at your motel and contact the stud's owner first thing in the morning. If possible, leave children and relatives at home, as they will only be in the way and perhaps unwelcome by the stud's owner. Most stud dog owners prefer not to have any unnecessary people on hand during the actual mating.

After the breeding has taken place, if you wish to sit and visit for awhile and the stud's owner has the time,

return the bitch to her crate in your car (first ascertaining, of course, that the temperature is comfortable for her and that there is proper ventilation). She should not be permitted to urinate for at least one hour following the breeding. This is the time when you attend to the business part of the transaction. Pay the stud fee, upon which you should receive your breeding certificate and, if you do not already have it, a copy of the stud dog's pedigree. The owner of the stud dog does not sign or furnish a litter registration application until the puppies have been born.

Upon your return home, you can settle down and plan in happy anticipation a wonderful litter of puppies. A word of caution! Remember that although she has been bred, your bitch is still an interesting target for all male dogs, so guard her carefully for the next week or until you are absolutely certain that her season has entirely ended. This would be no time to have any unfortunate incident with another dog.

THE STUD DOG

Choosing the best stud dog to complement your bitch is often very difficult. The two principal factors to be considered should be the stud's conformation and his pedigree. Conformation is fairly obvious; you want a dog that is typical of the breed in the words of the Standard of perfection. Understanding pedigrees is a bit more subtle since the pedigree lists the ancestry of the dog and involves individuals and bloodlines with which you may not be entirely familiar.

To a novice in the breed, the correct interpretation of a pedigree may at first be difficult to grasp. Study the pictures and text of this book and you will find many names of important bloodlines and members of the breed. Also make an effort to discuss the various dogs behind the proposed stud with some of the more experienced breeders, starting with the breeder of your own bitch. Frequently these folks will be familiar with many of the dogs in question, will be able to offer opinions of them, and may have access to additional pictures which you would benefit by seeing. It is very

The Stud Dog Class at Montgomery County in 1982. *On the left,* the sire is **Ch. Skaket's Candy Man, U.D.T., T.T.,** owned by Nancy and Mitzi Gauthier. *Center,* **Ch. Battle Road Maud Moon,** daughter of Candy Man from Lonsdale Scotch Mist; owner Joan Reddy, who is also co-breeder with Patricia Storey. *Right,* **Ch. Lonsdale Cass,** also by Candy Man from Scotch Mist, owned by Patricia Storey, the co-breeder with Joan Reddy.

important that the stud's pedigree be harmonious with that of the bitch you plan on breeding to him. Do not rush out and breed to the latest winner with no thought of whether or not he can produce true quality. By no means are all great show dogs great producers. It is the producing record of the dog in question, and the dogs and bitches from which he has come, that should be the basis on which you make your choice.

Breeding dogs is never a money-making operation. By the time you pay a stud fee, care for the bitch during pregnancy, whelp the litter, and rear the puppies through their early shots, worming, and so on, you will be fortunate to break even financially once the puppies have been sold. Your chances of doing this are greater if you are breeding for a show-quality litter which will bring you higher prices, as the pups are sold as show prospects. Therefore, your wisest investment is to use the best dog available for your bitch regardless of the cost; then you should wind up with more valuable puppies. Remember that it is equally costly to raise mediocre puppies as it is top ones, and your chances of financial return are better on the latter. Breeding to the most excellent, most suitable stud dog you can find is the only sensible thing to do, and it is poor economy to quibble over the amount you are paying in a stud fee.

It will be your decision as to which course you follow when you breed your bitch, as there are three options: linebreeding, inbreeding, and outcrossing. Each of these methods has its supporters and its detractors! Linebreeding is breeding a bitch to a dog belonging originally to the same canine family, being descended from the

Ch. Glengidge Pickpocket is the litter brother to Ch. Glengidge Easy Virtue, taking the first of back-to-back "majors" at Somerset Hills K.C. en route to his championship. The judge was Heywood Hartley. Seymour Weiss handling for himself and co-owner Helene Weiss.

same ancestors, such as half-brother to half-sister, grandsire to granddaughter, niece to uncle (and vice-versa) or cousin to cousin. Inbreeding is breeding father to daughter, mother to son, or full-brother to sister. Outcross breeding is breeding a dog and a bitch with no or only a few mutual ancestors.

Linebreeding is probably the safest course, and the one most likely to bring results, for the novice breeder. The more sophisticated inbreeding should be left to the experienced, longtime breeders who throroughly know and understand the risks and the possibilities involved with a particular line. It is usually done in an effort to intensify some ideal feature in that strain. Outcrossing is the reverse of inbreeding, an effort to introduce improvement in a specific feature needing correction, such as a shorter back, better movement, more correct head or coat, and so on.

It is the serious breeder's ambition to develop a strain or bloodline of their own, one strong in qualities for which their dogs will become distinguished. However, it must be realized that this will involve time, patience, and at least several generations before the achievement can be claimed. The safest way to embark on this plan, as previously mentioned, is by the selection and breeding of one or two bitches, the best you can buy and from top-producing kennels. In the beginning you do *not* really have to own a stud dog. In the long run it is less expensive and sounder judgement to pay a stud fee when you are ready

Ch. Kilkerran N' Wicket A Kut Above, co-owner-handled by Nancy Spelke of Pasadena, CA, winning an important Westie specialty. Kutter is owned by Nancy Spelke with breeder Kathleen Kompare and Laura Moreno.

to breed a bitch than to purchase a stud dog and feed him all year; a stud dog does not win any popularity contests with owners of bitches to be bred until he becomes a champion, has been successfully Specialed for a while, and has been at least moderately advertised, all of which adds up to quite a healthy expenditure.

The wisest course for the inexperienced breeder just starting out in dogs is to keep the best bitch puppy

The foundation bitch at Carolyn Gardner's kennel in Closter, NJ. **Ch. MacSkathll's Lady Harrison,** a daughter of Ch. Braidholmes White Tornado of Binate ex Kiloran Lea Kera Kildoran.

from the first several litters. After that you may wish to consider keeping your own stud dog, if there has been a particularly handsome male in one of your litters that you feel has great potential or if you know where there is one available that you are interested in, with the feeling that he would work in nicely with the breeding program on which you have embarked. By this time, with several litters already born, your eye should have developed to a point enabling you to make a wise choice, either from one of your own litters or from among dogs you have

seen that appear suitable.

The greatest care should be taken in the selection of your own stud dog. He must be of true type and highest quality as he may be responsible for siring many puppies each year, and he should come from a line of excellent dogs on both sides of his pedigree which themselves are, and which are descended from, successful producers. This dog should have no glaring faults in conformation; he should be of such quality that he can hold his own in keenest competition within his breed. He should be in good health, be virile and be a keen stud dog, a proven sire able to transmit his correct qualities to his puppies. Need one say that such a dog will be enormously expensive unless you have the good fortune to produce him in one of your own litters? To buy and use a lesser stud dog, however, is downgrading your breeding program unnecessarily since there are so many dogs fitting the description of a fine stud whose services can be used on payment of a stud fee.

You should never breed to an unsound dog or one with any serious disqualifying faults according to the breed's standard. Not all champions by any means pass along their best features; and by the same token, occasionally you will find a great one who can pass along his best features but never gained his championship title due to some unusual circumstances. The information you need about a stud dog is what type of puppies he has produced, and with what bloodlines, and whether or not he possesses the bloodlines and attributes considered characteristic of the best in your breed.

If you go out to buy a stud dog, obviously he will not be a puppy, but rather a fully mature and proven male with as many of the best attributes as possible. True, he will be an expensive investment, but if you choose and make his selection with care and forethought, he may well prove to be one of the best investments you have ever made.

Of course, the most exciting of all is when a young male you have decided to keep from one of your litters, due to his tremendous show potential, turns out to be a stud dog such as we have described. In this case he should be managed with care, for he is a valuable property that can contribute inestimably to this breed as a whole and to your own kennel specifically.

Do not permit your stud dog to be used until he is about a year old, and even then he should be bred to a mature, proven matron accustomed to breeding who will make his first experience pleasant and easy. A young dog can be put off forever by a maiden bitch who fights and resists his advances. Never allow this to happen. Always start a stud dog out with a bitch who is mature, has been bred previously, and is of even temperament. The first breeding should be performed in quiet surroundings with only you

Best of Winners, Westchester K.C. 1984. **Ch. Mac-Ken-Char's Ms. Mariner** taking Winners Bitch and Best of Winners from the 6–9-Month Puppy Class at the WHWTC of Greater NY Specialty. Sired by Ch. Mac-Ken-Char's Irish Navigator ex Ch. Msbysen O'The Ridge, this lovely bitch is a Jenny Jump Up granddaughter. Breeders and owners, Marjadele Schiele and Jaimi and Joanne Glodek.

and one other person to hold the bitch. Do not make it a circus, as the experience will determine the dog's outlook about future stud work. If he does not enjoy the first experience or associates it with any unpleasantness, you may well have a problem in the future.

Your young stud must permit help with the breeding, as later there will be bitches who will not be cooperative. If right from the beginning you are there helping him and praising him, whether or not your assistance is actually needed, he will expect and accept this as a matter of course when a difficult bitch comes along.

Things to have handy before introducing your dog and the bitch are K-Y jelly (the only lubricant which should be used) and a length of gauze with which to muzzle the bitch should it be necessary to keep her from biting you or the dog. Some bitches put up a fight; others are calm. It is best to be prepared.

At the time of the breeding, the stud fee comes due, and it is expected that it will be paid promptly. Normally a return service is offered in case the bitch misses or fails to produce one live puppy. Conditions of the service are what the stud dog's owner makes them, and there are no standard rules covering this. The stud fee is paid for the act, not the result. If the bitch fails to conceive, it is customary for the owner

Ch. Belash Bachelor Boy at Tervin, by Arnholme Aces High ex Belash Isha was bred by Mrs. I. Bell and owned by Mr. and Mrs. George H. Seemann, Jr., South Norwalk, CT. Here winning the Terrier Group at Bryn Mawr in 1986, handled by Cliff Hallmark.

to offer a free return service; but this is a courtesy and not to be considered a right, particularly in the case of a proven stud who is siring consistently and whose fault the failure obviously is *not*. Stud dog owners are always anxious to see their clients get good value and to have, in the ring, winning young stock by their dog; therefore, very few refuse to mate the second time. It is wise, however, for both parties to have the terms of the transaction clearly understood at the time of the breeding.

If the return service has been provided and the bitch has missed a second time, that is considered to be the end of the matter and the owner would be expected to pay a further fee if it is felt that the bitch should be given a third chance with the stud dog. The management of a stud dog and his visiting bitches is quite a task, and a stud fee has usually been well earned when one service has been achieved, let alone by repeated visits from the same bitch.

The accepted litter is one live puppy. It is wise to have printed a breeding certificate which the owner of the stud dog and the owner of the bitch both sign. This should list in detail the conditions of the breeding as well as the dates of the mating.

Upon occasion, arrangements other than a stud fee in cash are made for a breeding, such as the owner of the stud taking a pick-of-the-litter puppy in lieu of money. This should be clearly specified on the breeding certificate along with the terms of the age at which the

Ch. Bel-West Taco Belle, a daughter of Ch. Mac-Ken-Char's Navigator ex Ch. Olac Moon Penny of Bel-West, is taking Best of Opposite Sex at the 1989 Great Western Specialty. Bred and owned by Maura and Harold Heubel, Phoenix, AZ, handled by Harold Heubel.

stud's owner will select the puppy, whether it is to be a specific sex, or whether it is to be the pick of the entire litter.

The price of a stud fee varies according to circumstances. Usually, to prove a young stud dog, his owner will allow the first breeding to

LOUISIANA KC
BEST IN SHOW

Ch. Snowbank Starr Shine, a son of Ch. Round Town Duke J. Ellington, taking Best in Show at the Louisiana K.C. in 1987. Photo courtesy of Amelia and Dan Musser, Laingsburg, MI. Roz Kraus, handler.

champions starts to grow, so does the amount of the stud fee. For a top-producing sire of champions, the stud fee will rise accordingly.

Almost invariably it is the bitch who comes to the stud dog for the breeding. Immediately upon having selected the stud dog you wish to use, discuss the possibility with the owner of that dog. It is the stud dog owner's prerogative to refuse to breed any bitch deemed unsuitable for this dog. Stud fee and method of payment should be stated at this time and a decision reached on whether it is to be a full cash transaction at the time of the mating or a pick-of-the-litter puppy, usually at eight weeks of age.

If the owner of the stud dog must travel to an airport to meet the bitch and ship her for the flight home, an additional charge will be made for time, tolls, and gasoline based on the stud owner's proximity to the airport. The stud fee includes board for the day on the bitch's arrival through two days for breeding, with a day in between. If it is necessary that the bitch remain longer, it is very likely that additional board will be charged at the normal per-day rate for the breed.

Be sure to advise the stud's owner

be quite inexpensive. Then, once a bitch has become pregnant by him, he becomes a "proven stud" and the fee rises accordingly for bitches that follow. The sire of championship quality puppies will bring a stud fee of at least the purchase price of one show puppy as the accepted "rule-of-thumb." Until at least one champion by your stud dog has finished, the fee will remain equal to the price of one pet puppy. When his list of as soon as you know that your bitch is in season so that the stud dog will be available. This is especially important because if he is a dog being shown, he and his owner may be unavailable, owing to the dog's absence from home.

As the owner of a stud dog being offered to the public, it is essential that you have proper facilities for the care of visiting bitches. Nothing can be worse than a bitch being insecurely housed and slipping out to become lost or bred by the wrong dog. If you are taking people's valued bitches into your kennel or home, it is imperative that you provide them with comfortable, secure housing and good care while they are your responsibility.

There is no dog more valuable than the proven sire of champions, Group winners, and Best in Show dogs. Once you have such an animal, guard his reputation well and do *not* permit him to be bred to just any bitch that comes along. It takes two to make the puppies; even the most dominant stud cannot do it all himself, so never permit him to breed a bitch you consider unworthy. Remember that when the puppies arrive, it will be your stud dog who will be blamed for any lack of quality, while the bitch's shortcomings will

Ch. Sno-Bilt's Notorious en route to the title taking points in 1989. Sired by Am. and Can. Ch. Sno-Bilt's Eliminator ex Ch. Heritage Phoebe's Pat O'Puzzle. Jodine Vertuno, owner, Sno-Bilt Kennels.

Ch. Lonsdale Moonbeam, by Ch. Jennessey's Myney ex Roseneath New Moon, en route to the title, owner-handled by Patricia P. Storey.

Ch. Donnybrook's Eve, by Ch. Donnybrook's Benjamin ex Ch. Whitebriar Jolliminx, foundation of the current line at Glengidge Kennels, Helene and Seymour Weiss.

If you get a complete tie, probably only the one mating is absolutely necessary. However, especially with a maiden bitch or one that has come a long distance for this breeding, a follow-up with a second breeding is preferred, leaving one day in between the two matings. In this way there will be little or no chance of the bitch missing.

Once the tie has been completed and the dogs release, be certain that the male's penis goes completely back within its sheath. He should be allowed a drink of water and a short walk, and then he should be put into his crate or somewhere alone where he can settle down. Do not allow him to be with other dogs for a while as they will notice the odor of the bitch on him, and, particularly with other males present, he may become involved in a fight.

PREGNANCY, WHELPING, AND THE LITTER

Once the bitch has been bred and is back at home, remember to keep an ever watchful eye that no other males get to her until at least the twenty-second day of her season has passed. Until then, it will still be possible for an unwanted breeding

be quickly and conveniently overlooked.

Going into the actual management of the mating is a bit superfluous here. If you have had previous experience in breeding a dog and bitch, you will know how the mating is done. If you do not have such experience, you should not attempt to follow directions given in a book but should have a veterinarian, breeder friend, or handler there to help you with the first few times. You do not turn the dog and bitch loose together and await developments, as too many things can go wrong and you may altogether miss getting the bitch bred. Someone should hold the dog and the bitch (one person each) until the "tie" is made and these two people should stay with them during the entire act.

to take place, which at this point would be catastrophic. Remember that she actually can have two separate litters by two different dogs, so take care.

In other ways, she should be treated normally. Controlled exercise is good and necessary for the bitch throughout her pregnancy, tapering it off to just several short walks daily, preferably on lead, as she reaches her seventh week. As her time grows close, be careful about her jumping or playing too roughly.

The theory that a bitch should be overstuffed with food when pregnant is a poor one. A fat bitch is never an easy whelper, so the overfeeding you consider good for her may well turn out to be a hindrance later on. During the first few weeks of pregnancy, your bitch should be fed her normal diet. At four to five weeks along, calcium should be added to her food. At seven weeks her food may be increased if she seems to crave more than she is getting, and a meal of canned milk (mixed with an equal amount of water) should be introduced. If she is fed just once a day, add another meal rather than overload her with too much at one time. If twice a day is her schedule, then a bit more food can be added to each feeding.

A week before the pups are due, your bitch should be introduced to her whelping box so that she will be accustomed to it and feel at home there when the puppies arrive. She should be encouraged to sleep there but permitted to come and go as she wishes. The box should be roomy enough for her to lie down and stretch out in

Ch. D'Alexa's Mister Mac-Ken-Char, by Ch. Donnybrook's Benjamin ex Ch. Mac-Ken-Char's Mariposa, owned by Joanne and Jaimi Glodek, Severn, MD.

but not too large, lest the pups have more room than is needed in which to roam and possibly get chilled by going too far away from their mother. Be sure that the box has a "pig rail"; this will prevent the puppies from being crushed against the sides The room in which the box is placed, either in your home or in the kennel, should be kept at about 70 degrees Fahrenheit. In winter it may be necessary to have an infrared lamp over the whelping box, in which case be careful not to place it too low or close to the puppies.

Newspapers will become a very important commodity, so start collecting them well in advance to have a big pile handy for the whelping box. With a litter of puppies, one never seems to have papers enough, so the higher pile to start with, the better off you will be. Other necessities for whelping time are clean, soft turkish towels, scissors, and a bottle of alcohol.

You will know that her time is very near when your bitch becomes restless, wandering in and out of her box and out of the room. She may refuse food, and at that point her temperature will start to drop. She will dig at and tear up the newspapers in her box, shiver, and generally look uncomfortable. Only you should be with your bitch at this time. She does not need spectators; and several people hanging over her, even though they may be family members whom she knows, may upset her to the point where she may harm the puppies. You should remain nearby, quietly watching, not fussing or hovering;

speak calmly and frequently to her to instill confidence. Eventually she will settle down in her box and begin panting; contractions will follow. Soon thereafter a puppy will start to emerge, sliding out with the contractions. The mother immediately should open the sac, sever the cord with her teeth, and then clean up the puppy. She will also eat the placenta, which you should permit. Once the puppy is cleaned, it should be placed next to the bitch unless she is showing signs of having the next one immediately. Almost at once the puppy will start looking for a nipple on which to nurse, and you should ascertain that it is able to latch on successfully.

If the puppy is a breech (*i.e.*, born feet first), you must watch carefully for it to be completely delivered as quickly as possible and for the sac to be removed quickly so that the puppy does not drown. Sometimes even a normally positioned birth will seem extremely slow in coming. Should this occur, you might take a clean towel, and as the bitch contracts, pull the puppy out, doing so gently and with utmost care. If, once the puppy is delivered, it shows little signs of life, take a rough turkish towel and massage the puppy's chest by rubbing quite briskly back and forth. Continue this for about fifteen minutes, and be sure that the mouth is free of liquid. It may be necessary to try mouth-to-mouth breathing, which is begun by pressing the puppy's jaws open and, using a finger, depressing the tongue which may be stuck to the roof of the mouth. Then place your mouth against the puppy's and blow hard down the puppy's throat. Rub the puppy's chest with the towel again and try artificial respiration, pressing the sides of the chest together slowly and rhythmically—in and out, in and out. Keep trying one method or the other for at least twenty minutes before giving up. You may be rewarded with a live puppy who otherwise would not have made it.

If you are successful in bringing the puppy around, do not immediately put it back with the mother as it should be kept extra warm. Put it in a cardboard box on an electric heating pad or, if it is the time of year when your heat is running, near a radiator or near the fireplace or stove. As soon as the rest of the litter has been born, it then can join the others.

An hour or more may elapse between puppies, which is fine so long as the bitch seems comfortable and is neither straining nor contracting. She should not be permitted to remain unassisted for more than an hour if she does continue to contract. This is when you should get her to your veterinarian, whom you should already have alerted to the possibility of a problem existing. He should examine her and perhaps give her a shot of Pituitrin. In some

"Sweet dreams". This is **Manley** as a baby puppy at Shelly Bay at the home of his breeder Marilyn Foster.

cases the veterinarian may find that a Caesarean section is necessary due to a puppy being lodged in a manner making normal delivery impossible. Sometimes this is caused by an abnormally large puppy, or it may just be that the puppy is simply turned in the wrong position. If the bitch does require a Caesarean section, the puppies already born must be kept warm in their cardboard box with a heating pad under the box.

Once the section is done, get the bitch and the puppies home. Do not attempt to put the puppies in with the bitch until she has regained consciousness, as she may unknowingly hurt them. But do get them back to her as soon as possible for them to start nursing.

Should the mother lack milk at this time, the puppies must be fed by hand, kept very warm, and held onto the mother's teats several times a day in order to stimulate and encourage the secretion of milk, which should start shortly.

Assuming that there has been no problem and that the bitch has whelped naturally, you should insist that she go out to exercise, staying just long enough to make herself comfortable. She can be offered a bowl of milk and a biscuit, but then she should settle down with her family. Freshen the whelping box for her with newspapers while she is taking this respite so that she and the puppies will have a clean bed.

Unless some problem arises, there is little you must do for the puppies until they become three to four weeks old. Keep the box clean and supplied with fresh newspapers the first few days, but then turkish towels should be tacked down to the bottom of the box so that the puppies will have traction as they move about.

If the bitch has difficulties with her milk supply, or if you should be so unfortunate as to lose her, then you must be prepared to either hand-feed or tube-feed the puppies if they are to survive. Tube-feeding is so much faster and easier. If the bitch is available, it is best that she continues to clean and care for the puppies in the normal manner, excepting for the food supplements you will provide. If it is impossible for her to do this, then after every feeding you must gently rub each puppy's abdomen with wet cotton to make it urinate, and the rectum should be gently rubbed to open the bowels.

Newborn puppies must be fed every three to four hours around the clock. The puppies must be kept warm during this time. Have your veterinarian teach you how to tube-feed. You will find that it is really quite simple.

After a normal whelping, the bitch will require additional food to enable her to produce sufficient milk. In addition to being fed twice daily, she should be given some canned milk several times each day.

When the puppies are two weeks old, their nails should be clipped, as they are needle sharp at this age and can hurt or damage the mother's teats and stomach as the pups hold on to nurse.

Between three and four weeks of age, the puppies should begin to be weaned. Scraped beef (prepared by scraping it off slices of beef with a spoon so that none of the gristle is included) may be offered in very small quantities a couple of times daily for the first few days. Then by the third day you can mix puppy chow with warm water as directed on the package, offering it four times daily. By now the mother should be kept away from the puppies and out of the box for several hours at a time so that when they have reached five weeks of age she is left in with them only overnight. By the time the puppies are six weeks old, they should be entirely weaned and receiving only occasional visits from their mother.

Most veterinarians recommend a temporary DHL (distemper, hepatitis, leptospirosis) shot when the puppies are six weeks of age. This remains effective for about two weeks. Then at eight weeks of age, the puppies should receive the series of permanent shots for DHL

These two adorable nine-week-old Westie babies are by Best in Show Ch. Sno-Bilt's Puzzle ex Ch. Gardner's Blk Eye Susan Orion. Owned by Carolyn Gardner.

protection. It is also a good idea to discuss with your vet the advisability of having your puppies inoculated against the dreaded parvovirus at the same time. Each time the pups go to the vet for shots, you should bring stool samples so that they can be examined for worms.

Worms go through various stages of development and may be present in a stool sample even though the sample does not test positive in every checkup. So do not neglect to keep careful watch on this.

The puppies should be fed four times daily until they are three months old. Then you can cut back to three feedings daily. By the time the puppies are six months of age, two meals daily are sufficient. Some people feed their dogs twice daily throughout their lifetime; others go to one meal daily when the puppy becomes one year of age.

The ideal age for puppies to go to their new homes is between eight and twelve weeks, although some puppies successfully adjust to a new home when they are six weeks old. Be sure that they go to their new owners accompanied by a description of the diet you've been feeding them and a schedule of the shots they have already received and those they still need. These should be included with the registration application and a copy of the pedigree.

A six-week-old puppy of exceptional promise, **Crinan Christmas Sno** shows us the quality breeders like to see at this precious age.

Starting to shape up at age 15 weeks. **Crinan Christmas Sno** has obviously been "learning the ropes". Note the excellent length of neck, shortness of back, well developing head and obvious soundness of this exciting puppy.

The Making of a Show Dog

If you have decided to become a show dog exhibitor, you have accepted a very real and very exciting challenge. The groundwork has been accomplished with the selection of your future show prospect. If you have purchased a puppy, it is assumed that you have gone through all the proper preliminaries concerning good care, which should be the same if the puppy is a pet or future show dog, with a few added precautions for the latter.

GENERAL CONSIDERATIONS

Remember the importance of keeping your future winner in trim, top condition. Since you want him neither too fat nor too thin, his appetite for his proper diet should be guarded, and children and guests should not be permitted to constantly feed him "goodies." The best treat of all is a small wad of raw ground beef or a packaged dog treat. To be avoided are ice cream, cake, cookies, potato chips, and other fattening items which will cause the dog to put on weight and may additionally spoil his appetite for the proper, nourishing, well-balanced diet so essential to good health and condition.

The importance of temperament and showmanship cannot possibly be overestimated. They have put many a mediocre dog across, while lack of them can ruin the career of an otherwise outstanding specimen. From the day your dog joins your family, socialize him. Keep him accustomed to being with people and to being handled by people. Encourage your friends and relatives to "go over" him as the judges will in the ring so this will not seem a strange and upsetting experience.

Ch. Whitebriar Jollimont with handler Dora Lee Wilson. Nicely set up on the table for inspection by the judge.

Practice showing his "bite" (the manner in which his teeth meet) quickly and deftly. It is quite simple to slip the lips apart with your fingers, and the puppy should be willing to accept this from you or the judge without struggle.

Some judges prefer that the exhibitors display the dog's bite and other mouth features themselves. These are the considerate ones, who do not wish to chance the spreading of possible infection from dog to dog with their hands on each one's

This photo from Montgomery County 1985 is a general view of the 6-9-Month Puppy Dog Class at this most famed Terrier classic. Judge, Peggy J. Haas, here is examining **Raglan Ragtime Jimmy Cagney** handled by the noted Canadian professional handler Luke Erlick. Photo courtesy of Joan Zwicker.

mouth—a courtesy particularly appreciated in these days of virus epidemics. But the old-fashioned judges still persist in doing it themselves, so the dog should be ready for either possibility.

Take your future show dog with you in the car, thus accustoming him to riding so that he will not become carsick on the day of a dog show. He should associate pleasure and attention with going in the car, van, or motor home. Take him where it is crowded: downtown, to the shops, everywhere you go that dogs

are permitted. Make the expeditions fun for him by frequent petting and words of praise; do not just ignore him as you go about your errands.

Do not overly shelter your future show dog. Instinctively you may want to keep him at home where he is safe from germs or danger. This can be foolish on two counts. The first reason is that a puppy kept away from other dogs builds up no natural immunity against all the things with which he will come in contact at dog shows, so it is wiser to keep him up-to-date on all protective shots and then let him become accustomed to being among dogs and dog owners. Also, a dog who is never among strange people, in strange places, or among strange dogs may grow up with a shyness or timidity of spirit that will cause you real problems as his show career draws near.

Keep your show prospect's coat in immaculate condition with frequent grooming and daily brushing. When bathing is necessary, use a mild dog shampoo or whatever the breeder of your puppy may suggest. Several of the brand-name products do an excellent job. Be sure to rinse thoroughly so as not to risk skin irritation by traces of soap left behind, and protect against soap entering the eyes by a drop of castor oil in each before you lather up. Use warm water (be sure it is not uncomfortably hot or chillingly cold) and a good spray. Make certain you allow your dog to dry thoroughly in a warm, draft-free area (or outdoors, if it is warm and sunny) so that he doesn't catch cold. Then proceed to groom him to perfection.

A show dog's teeth must be kept clean and free of tartar. Hard dog biscuits can help toward this, but if tartar accumulates, see that it is removed promptly by your veterinarian. Bones for chewing are not suitable for show dogs as they tend to damage and wear down the tooth enamel.

Assuming that you will be handling the dog yourself, or even if he will be professionally handled, a few moments each day of dog show routine is important. Practice setting him up as you have seen the exhibitors do at the shows you've attended, and teach him to hold this position once you have him stacked to your satisfaction. Make the learning period pleasant by being firm but lavish in your praise when he responds correctly. Teach him to gait at your side at a moderate rate on a loose lead. When you have mas-

tered the basic essentials at home, then hunt out and join a training class for future work. Training classes are sponsored by show-giving clubs in many areas, and their popularity is steadily increasing. If you have no other way of locating one, perhaps your veterinarian would know of one through some of his other clients; but if you are sufficiently aware of the dog show world to want a show dog, you will probably be personally acquainted with other people who will share information of this type with you.

Accustom your show dog to being in a crate (which you should be doing with a pet dog as well). He should relax in his crate at the

Surrounded by the "booty" from a successful specialty winning day, **Ch. Dawn's Moment 'N' Time** is a proudly owned homebred belonging to Dawn L. Martin and Patricia Parks. Sired by the noted Ch. Biljonblue's Best of Times ex Ch. Dawn's Vivacious Vivian, this notable young Westie is handled by Dawn Martin. Do note all the handsome Westie figurines in this photo. Westies are extremely popular with the artists who feature dog breeds in their collections, adding to the fun of collecting as a side hobby!

Ch. Gardner's Blk Eye Susan Orion taking a Group Second from judge Ron Krohne at Union County K.C., May 1989. Carolyn Gardner, owner, Closter, NJ.

shows "between times" for his own well being and safety.

MATCH SHOWS

Your show dog's initial experience in the ring should be in match show competition. This type of event is intended as a learning experience for both the dog and the exhibitor. You will not feel embarrassed or out of place no matter how poorly your puppy may behave or how inept your attempts at handling may be, as you will find others there with the same type of problems. The important thing is that you get the puppy out and into a show ring where the two of you can practice together and learn the ropes.

Only on rare occasions is it necessary to make match show entries in advance, and even those with a pre-entry policy will usually accept entries at the door as well. Thus you need not plan several weeks ahead, as is the case with point shows, but can go when the mood strikes you. Also there is a vast difference in the cost, as match show entries only cost a few dollars while entry fees for the point shows may be over ten dollars, an amount none of us needs to waste until we have some idea of how the puppy will behave or how much more pre-show training is needed.

Match shows are frequently judged by professional handlers who, in addition to making the awards, are happy to help new exhibitors with comments and advice on their puppies and their presentation of them. Avail yourself of all these opportunities before heading out to the sophisticated world of the point shows.

POINT SHOWS

Point shows are essentially an American and Continental convention. The process and classes in England are entirely different. Entries for American Kennel Club point shows must be made in advance. This must be done on an official entry blank of the show-giving club. The entry must then be filed either personally or by mail with the show superintendent or the show secretary (if the event is being run by the club members alone and a superintendent has not been hired, this information will appear on the premium list) in time to reach its destination prior to the published closing date or filling of

Ch. Gardner's Blossom Plenty, by Am. and Can. Ch. Gardner's Frst Bud O' Mauradoon ex Ch. Gardner's Morning Glory. Owned by Carolyn Gardner.

Ch. Glengidge Birthday Promise, by Ch. Glengidge Pickpocket ex Ch. Glengidge Candy Kiss. "Ruffie" earned her championship from the Bred-by Exhibitor Class, owner-handler Seymour Weiss, co-owner with Helene Weiss.

the name of the new owner in any show for which entries close after the date of acquirement, regardless of whether the new owner has or has not actually received the registration certificate indicating that the dog is recorded in his name. State on the entry form whether or not transfer application has been mailed to the American Kennel Club, and it goes without saying that the latter should be attended to promptly when you purchase a registered dog.

the quota. These entries must be made carefully, must be signed by the owner of the dog or the owner's agent (your professional handler), and must be accompanied by the entry fee; otherwise they will not be accepted. Remember that it is not when the entry leaves your hands that counts, but the date of arrival at its destination. If you are relying on the mails, which are not always dependable, get the entry off well before the deadline to avoid disappointment.

A dog must be entered at a dog show in the name of the actual owner at the time of the entry closing date of that specific show. If a registered dog has been acquired by a new owner, it must be entered in

In filling out your entry blank, type, print, or write clearly, paying particular attention to the spelling of names, correct registration numbers, and so on. Also, if there is more than one variety in your breed, be sure to indicate into which category your dog is being entered.

The **Puppy Class** is for dogs or bitches who are six months of age and under twelve months and who are not champions. The age of a dog shall be calculated up to and inclusive of the first day of a show. For example, the first day a dog whelped on January 1st is eligible to compete in a Puppy Class at a show is July 1st of the same year; and he may continue to compete in Puppy Classes up to and including a show on December 31 of the same year, but he is *not* eligible to compete in a Puppy Class at a show held on or after January 1 of the following year.

The Puppy Class is the first one in which you should enter your puppy. In it a certain allowance will be made for the fact that they *are* puppies, thus an immature dog or one displaying less than perfect showmanship will be less severely penalized than, for instance, would be the case in Open. It is also quite likely that others in the class will be suffering from these problems, too. When you enter a puppy, be sure to check the classification with care, as some shows divide their Puppy Class into a 6-9 months old section and a 9-12 months old section.

The **Novice Class** is for dogs six months of age and over, whelped in the United States or Canada, who *prior to the official closing date for entries* have *not* won three first prizes in the Novice Class, any first prize at all in the Bred-by-Exhibitor, American-bred, or Open Classes, or one or more points toward championship. The provisions for this class are confusing to many people, which is probably the reason exhibitors do not enter in it more frequently. A dog may win any number of first prizes in the Puppy Class and still

retain his eligibility for Novice. He may place second, third, or fourth not only in Novice on an unlimited number of occasions, but also in Bred-by-Exhibitor, American-bred and Open and still remain eligible

Montgomery County 1988. In the holding area (where dogs entered for the next class wait for the judge to complete the one under way in order to promptly enter the ring) is the great **Ch. Skaket's Candy Man** greeting his daughter, **Bar-Dan's Hershey's Kisses** *(on the left)*, the latter owned by Barbara A. Krotts and M. Harness.

for Novice. But he may no longer be shown in Novice when he has won three blue ribbons in that class, when he has won even one blue ribbon in either Bred-by-Exhibitor, American-bred, or Open, or when he has won a single championship point.

In determining whether or not a dog is eligible for the Novice Class, keep in mind the fact that previous wins are calculated according to the official published date for closing of entries, not by the date on which

Ch. Lite N Lively's Hello Dolly, bred and owned by Mrs. Em Schoonover, was a well-known and successful winning daughter of Ch. Orion's Man in the Moon. Tom Natalini, handler.

it. The Novice Class always seems to have the fewest entries of any class, and therefore it is a splendid "practice ground" for you and your young dog while you are getting the "feel" of being in the ring.

Bred-by-Exhibitor Class is for dogs whelped in the United States or, if individually registered in the American Kennel Club Stud Book, for dogs whelped in Canada who are six months of age or older, are not champions, and are owned wholly or in part by the person or by the spouse of the person who was the breeder or one of the breeders of record. Dogs entered in this class must be handled in the class by an owner or by a member of the immediate family of the owner. Members of an immediate family for this purpose are husband, wife, father, mother, son, daughter, brother, or sister. This is the class which is really the "breeders' showcase," and the one which breeders should enter with particular pride to show off their achievements.

The **American-bred Class** is for all dogs excepting champions, six months of age or older, who were whelped in the United States by reason of a mating which took place in the United States.

The **Open Class** is for any dog six

you may actually have made the entry. So if in the interim, between the time you made the entry and the official closing date, your dog makes a win causing him to become ineligible for Novice, change your class *immediately* to another for which he will be eligible, preferably either Bred-by-Exhibitor or American-bred. To do this, you must contact the show's superintendent or secretary, at first by telephone to save time and then in writing to confirm months of age or older (this is the only restriction for this class). Dogs with championship points compete in it, dogs who are already champions are eligible to do so, dogs who are imported can be entered, and, of course, American-bred dogs compete in it. This class is, for some strange reason, the favorite of exhibitors who are "out to win." They rush to enter their pointed dogs in it, under the false impression that by doing so they assure themselves of greater attention from the judges. This really is not so, and some people feel that to enter in one of the less competitive classes, with a better chance of winning it and thus earning a second opportunity of gaining the judge's approval by returning to the ring in the Winners Class, can often be a more effective strategy.

One does not enter the **Winners Class.** One earns the right to compete in it by winning first prize in Puppy, Novice, Bred-by-Exhibitor, American-bred, or Open. No dog who has been defeated on the same day in one of these classes is eligible to compete for Winners, and every dog who has been a blue-ribbon winner in one of them and not defeated in another, should he have been entered in more than one class (as occasionally happens), *must* do so. Following the selection of the Winners Dog or the Winners Bitch, the dog or bitch receiving

that award leaves the ring. Then the dog or bitch who placed second in that class, unless previously beaten by another dog or bitch in another class at the same show, re-enters the ring to compete against the remaining first-prize winners for Reserve. The latter award indicates that the dog or bitch selected for it is standing "in reserve" should the

Ch. Royal Tartan Glen O'Red Lodge, one of the top sires in the breed, was a highly successful son of Ch. Elfinbrook Simon. Owned by Barbara W. Keenan, Wishing Wells Kennels.

one who received Winners be disqualified or declared ineligible through any technicality when the awards are checked at the American Kennel Club. In that case, the one who placed Reserve is moved up to Winners, at the same time receiving the appropriate championship points.

Winners Dog and Winners Bitch are the awards which carry points toward championship with them. The points are based on the number of dogs or bitches actually in competition, and the points are scaled

Close to the title, the lovely **Dalriada Rose Is A Rose.** Janis W. Chapman, owner, Dalriada Westie, Fairfax, VA. Rose is by Ch. Happiness Iss Harlee ex Happiness Iss Rowdee.

can Kennel Gazette, the official publication of the American Kennel Club.

The scale of championship points for each breed is worked out by the American Kennel Club and reviewed annually, at which time the number required in competition may be either changed (raised or lowered) or remain the same. The scale of championship points for all breeds is published annually in the May issue of the Gazette, and

one through five, the latter being the greatest number available to any one dog or bitch at any one show. Three-, four-, or five-point wins are considered majors. In order to become a champion, a dog or bitch must have won two majors under two different judges, plus at least one point from a third judge, and the additional points necessary to bring the total to fifteen. When your dog has gained fifteen points as described above, a championship certificate will be issued to you, and your dog's name will be published in the champions of record list in the *Pure-Bred Dogs / Ameri-*

the current ratings for each breed within that area are published in every show catalog.

When a dog or bitch is adjudged Best of Winners, its championship points are, for that show, compiled on the basis of which sex had the greater number of points. If there are two points in dogs and four in bitches and the dog goes Best of Winners, then *both* the dog and the bitch are awarded an equal number of points, in this case four. Should the Winners Dog or the Winners Bitch go on to win Best of Breed or Best of Variety, additional points are accorded for the additional dogs and bitches defeated by so doing, provided, of course, that there were entries specifically for Best of Breed competition or specials, as these specific entries are generally called.

If your dog or bitch takes Best of Opposite Sex after going Winners, points are credited according to the number of the same sex defeated in both the regular classes and Specials competition. If Best of Winners is also won, then whatever additional points for each of these awards are available will be credited. Many a one- or two-point win has grown into a major in this manner.

Moving further along, should your dog win its **Variety Group** from the classes (in other words, if it has taken either Winners Dog or Winners Bitch), you then receive points based on the greatest number of points awarded to any member of any breed included within that Group during that show's competition. Should the day's

winning also include Best in Show, the same rule of thumb applies, and your dog or bitch receives the highest number of points awarded to any other dog of any breed at that event.

Best of Breed competition consists of the Winners Dog and the Winners Bitch, who automatically

Ch. Pilot of Keithall is a distinguished British import owned by Martha W. Black of Washington Crossing, PA. Pilot is a Montgomery County Best of Breed winner with many other exciting successes to his credit in specialty and multiple-breed competition. He is handled by George Wright, was bred by Mrs. C.K. Bonas, and is a son of Ch. Exultation of Tasman ex Arnholme April Shower.

compete on the strength of those awards, in addition to whatever dogs and bitches have been entered specifically for this class for which champions of record are eligible. Since July 1980, dogs who, according to their owner's records, have completed the requirements for a championship after the closing of entries for the show (but whose championships are unconfirmed) may be transferred from one of the regular classes to the Best of Breed competition, provided this transfer is made by the show superintendent or show secretary *prior to the start of any judging at the show*.

This has proved an extremely popular new rule, as under it a dog can finish on Saturday and then be transferred and compete as a Special on Sunday. It must be emphasized that *the change must be made prior to the start of any part of the day's judging, not for just your individual breed.*

In the United States, Best of Breed winners are entitled to compete in the Variety Group which includes them. This is not mandatory; it is a privilege which exhibitors value. (In Canada,

Best of Breed winners *must* compete in the Variety Group or they lose any points already won.) The dogs winning *first* in each of the seven Variety Groups *must* compete for Best in Show. Missing the opportunity of taking your dog in for competition in its Group is foolish, as it is there where the general public is most likely to notice your breed and become interested in learning about it.

Non-regular classes are sometimes included at the all-breed shows, and they are almost invariably included at specialty shows. These include Stud Dog Class and Brood Bitch Class, which are judged on the basis of the quality of the two offspring accompanying the sire or dam. The quality of the latter two is beside the point and should not be considered by the judge; it is the youngsters who count, and the quality of *both* are to be averaged to decide which sire or dam is the best and most consistent producer. Then there is the Brace Class (which, at all-breed shows, moves up to Best Brace in each Variety Group and then Best Brace in

Cloudcroft's Punchline, bred and owned by Gale A. McDonald, Sutherlin, OR, is by Ch. Sno-Bilt's Puzzle ex Ch. Glenfinnan Proud As Punch, pictured winning Best in Sweepstakes at the Puget Sound Westie Specialty in August 1989, owner-handled.

Show) which is judged on the similarity and evenness of appearance of the two brace members. In other words, the two dogs should look like identical twins in size, color, and conformation and should move together almost as a single dog, one person handling with precision and ease. The same applies to the Team Class competition, except that four dogs are involved and, if necessary, two handlers.

The Veterans Class is for

This beautiful pair of Westies won Best Brace in Show at Montgomery County 1989, handled by 12-year-old Jonathan Marks, Jr., for owners Patricia H. Marks and breeder-co-owner Dawn L. Martin. *On the left,* **Dawn's Pride 'N' Joy.** *On the right,* **Dawn's Pard'n Me Boys.** Jonathan also handled "P.J." to a First in the large American-bred Class this same day.

Then there are Sweepstakes and Futurity Stakes sponsored by many Specialty clubs, sometimes as part of their regular Specialty shows and sometimes as separate events on an entirely different occasion. The difference between the two stakes is that Sweepstakes entries usually include dogs from six to eighteen months of age with entries made at the same time as the others for the show, while for a Fu-

the older dog, the minimum age of whom is seven years. This class is judged on the quality of the dogs, as the winner competes in Best of Breed competition and has, on a respectable number of occasions, been known to take that top award. So the point is *not* to pick out the oldest dog, as some judges seem to believe, but the best specimen of the breed, exactly as in the regular classes.

turity the entries are bitches nominated when bred and the individual puppies entered at or shortly following their birth.

JUNIOR SHOWMANSHIP COMPETITION

If there is a youngster in your family between the ages of ten and sixteen, there is no better or more rewarding hobby than becoming an

Ch. Dalriada I Can Do Magic, by Ch. Happiness Iss Harlee ex Happiness Iss Rowdee, belongs to Janis C. Chapman.

active participant in Junior Showmanship. This is a marvelous activity for young people. It teaches responsibility, good sportsmanship, the fun of competition where one's own skills are the deciding factor of success, proper care of a pet, and how to socialize with other young folks. Any youngster may experience the thrill of emerging from the ring a winner and the satisfaction of a good job well done.

Entry in Junior Showmanship Classes is open to any boy or girl who is at least ten years old and under seventeen years old on the day of the show. The Novice Junior Showmanship Class is open to youngsters who have not already won, at the time the entries close, three firsts in this class. Youngsters who have won three firsts in Novice may compete in the Open Junior Showmanship Class. Any junior handler who wins his third first-

place award in Novice may participate in the Open Class at the same show, provided that the Open Class has at least one other junior handler entered and competing in it that day. The Novice and Open Classes may be divided into Junior and Senior Classes. Youngsters between the ages of ten and twelve, inclusively, are eligible for the Junior division; and youngsters between thirteen and seventeen, inclusively, are eligible for the Senior division.

Any of the foregoing classes may be separated into individual classes for boys and for girls. If such a division is made, it must be so indicated on the premium list. The premium list also indicates the prize for Best Junior Handler, if such a prize is being offered at the show. Any youngster who wins a first in any of the regular classes may enter the competition for this prize, provided the youngster has been undefeated in any other Junior Showmanship Class at that show.

Junior Showmanship Classes, unlike regular conformation classes in which the quality of the dog is judged, are judged solely on the skill and ability of the junior handling the dog. Which dog is best is not the point—it is which youngster does the best job with the dog that is under consideration. Eligibility requirements for the dog being shown in Junior Showmanship, and other detailed information, can be found in *Regulations for Junior Showmanship*, available from the American Kennel Club.

A junior who has a dog that he or she can enter in both Junior Showmanship and conformation classes has twice the opportunity for success and twice the opportunity to get into the ring and work with the dog, a combination which can lead to not only awards for expert handling, but also, if the dog is of sufficient quality, for making a conformation champion.

PRE-SHOW PREPARATIONS

Preparation of the items you will need as a dog show exhibitor should not be left until the last moment. They should be planned and arranged several days in advance of the show in order for you to remain calm and relaxed as the countdown starts.

The importance of the crate has already been mentioned and should already be part of your equipment. Of equal importance is the grooming table, which very likely you have also already acquired for use at home. You should take it along with you to the shows, as your dog will need last minute touches before entering the ring. Should you have not yet made this purchase, folding tables with rubber tops are made specifically for this purpose and can be purchased at most dog shows, where concession booths with marvelous assortments of "doggy" necessities are to be found, or at your pet supplier. You will also need a sturdy tack box (also available at the dog show concessions) in which

to carry your grooming tools and equipment. The latter should include: brushes; combs; scissors; nail clippers; whatever you use for last minute clean-up jobs; cotton swabs; first-aid equipment; and anything you are in

Multiple Best in Show **Ch. Kilkerran Quintessence,** a "star" keeping his breed in the limelight under Nancy Spelke's handling for herself and Kathy Kompare who co-own this fabulous dog."Quin" was the nation's Number One Owner-handled Terrier in 1991.

the habit of using on the dog, including a leash or two of the type you prefer, some well-cooked and dried-out liver or any of the small packaged "dog treats" for use as bait in the ring, an atomizer in case you wish to dampen your dog's coat when you are preparing him for the ring, and so on. A large turkish towel to spread under

Ch. Kilkerran Name of the Game, by Ch. Whitebriar Jollimont ex Kilkerran Joy to the World, taking points towards the title in late 1989. Bred and owned by Kathy and Wayne Kompare, Danbury, CT.

the dog on the grooming table is also useful.

Take a large thermos or cooler of ice, the biggest one you can accommodate in your vehicle, for use by "man and beast." Take a jug of water (there are lightweight, inexpensive ones available at all sporting goods shops) and a water dish. If you plan to feed the dog at the show, or if you and the dog will be away from home more than one day, bring food for him from home so that he will have the type to which he is accustomed.

You may or may not have an exercise pen. While the shows do provide areas for exercise of the dogs, these are among the most likely places to have your dog come in contact with any illnesses which may be going around, and having a pen of your own for your dog's use is excellent protection. Such a pen comes in handy while you're traveling; since it is roomier than a crate, it becomes a comfortable place for your dog to relax and move around in, especially when you're at motels or rest stops. These pens are available at the show concession stands and come in a variety of heights and sizes. A set of "pooper scoopers" should also be part of your equipment, along with a package of plastic bags for cleaning up after your dog.

Bring along folding chairs for the members of your party, unless all of you are fond of standing, as these are almost never provided by the clubs. Have your name stamped on the chairs so that there will be no doubt as to whom the chairs belong. Bring whatever you and your family enjoy for drinks or snacks in a picnic basket or cooler, as show food, in general, is expensive and usually not great. You should always have a pair of boots, a raincoat, and a rain hat with you (they should remain permanently in your vehicle if you plan to attend shows regularly), as well as a sweater, a warm coat, and a change of shoes. A smock or big cover-up apron will assure that you remain tidy as you prepare the dog for the ring. Your overnight case should include a small sewing kit for emergency repairs, bandaids, headache and indigestion remedies, and any personal products or medica-

tions you normally use.

In your car, you should always carry maps of the area where you are headed and an assortment of motel directories. Generally speaking, Holiday Inns have been found to be the nicest about taking dogs. Ramadas and Howard Johnsons generally do so cheerfully (with a few exceptions). Best Western generally frowns on pets (not always, but often enough to make it necessary to find out which do). Some of the smaller chains welcome pets; the majority of privately-owned motels do not.

Have everything prepared the

Ch. Rudh'Re The Mac Neil, son of Ch. Whitebriar Jeronimo ex Rudh' Re Fennora, is a homebred owned by Joan Graber, Rudh'Re Westies, Middleton, WI.

night before the show to expedite your departure. Be sure that the dog's identification and your judging program and other show information are in your purse or briefcase. If you are taking sandwiches, have them ready. Anything that goes into the car the night before the show will be one thing less to remember in the morning. Decide upon what you will wear and have it out and ready. If there is any question in your mind about what to wear, try on the possibilities before the day of the show; don't risk feeling you may want to change when you see yourself dressed a few mo-

ments prior to departure time!

In planning your outfit, make it something simple that will not detract from your dog. Remember that a dark dog silhouettes attractively against a light background and viceversa. Sport clothes always seem to look best at dog shows, preferably conservative in type and not overly "loud" as you do not want to detract from your dog, who should be the focus of interest at this point. What you wear on your feet is important. Many types of flooring can be hazardously slippery, as can wet grass. Make it a habit to wear rubber soles and low or flat heels in the ring for

Multi-Best in Show and Group winner **Ch. Kilkerran Quintessence,** by Best in Show Ch. Kilkerran D'Artagnan ex Ch. Kilkerran Name of the Game, is a homebred co-owned by Kathy Kompare. This is a very youthful photo of Quin at the beginning of his show career.

your own safety, especially if you are showing a dog that likes to move out smartly.

Your final step in pre-show preparation is to leave yourself plenty of time to reach the show that morning. Traffic can get amazingly heavy as one nears the immediate area of the show, finding a parking place can be difficult, and other delays may occur. You'll be in better humor to enjoy the day if your trip to the show is not fraught with panic over fear of not arriving in time!

Ch. Kenstaff Saucy by Murrayisle Keppoch ex Murrayisle Powanthos. Here gaining points towards the title, Cliff Hallmark handling for Mr. and Mrs. George Seemann, Jr.

ENJOYING THE DOG SHOW

From the moment of your arrival at the show until after your dog has been judged, keep foremost in your mind the fact that he is your reason for being there and that he should therefore be the center of your attention. Arrive early enough to have time for those last-minute touches that can make a great difference when he enters the ring. Be sure that he has ample time to exercise and that he attends to personal matters. A dog arriving in the ring and immediately using it as an exercise pen hardly makes a favorable impression on the judge.

When you reach ringside, ask the steward for your arm-card and anchor it firmly into place on your arm. Make sure that you are where you should be when your class is called. The fact that you have picked up your arm-card does not guarantee, as some seem to think, that the judge will wait for you. The judge has a full schedule which he wishes to complete on time. Even though you may be nervous, assume an air of calm self-confidence. Remember that this is a hobby to be enjoyed, so approach it in that state of mind. The dog will do better, too, as he will be quick to reflect your attitude.

Always show your dog with an air of pride. If you make mistakes in presenting him, don't worry about it. Next time you will do better. Do not permit the presence of more experienced exhibitors to intimidate

213

Ch. Cleator's Cocksure, owned by Betty Lou Perridine, winning the very prestigious Terrier Group at the First Company Governors Foot Guard dog show, Hartford, CT, 1986. Handler, Chris C. Steele.

you. After all, they, too, were once newcomers.

The judging routine usually starts when the judge asks that the dogs be gaited in a circle around the ring. During this period the judge is watching each dog as it moves, noting style, topline, reach and drive, head and tail carriage, and general balance. Keep your mind and your eye on your dog, moving him at his most becoming gait and keeping your place in line without coming too close to the exhibitor ahead of you. Always keep your dog on the inside of the circle, between yourself and the judge, so that the judge's view of the dog is unobstructed.

Calmly pose the dog when requested to set up for examination. If you are at the head of the line and many dogs are in the class, go all the way to the end of the ring before starting to stack the dog, leaving sufficient space for those behind you to line theirs up as well, as requested by the judge. If you are not at the head of the line but between other exhibitors, leave sufficient space ahead of your dog for the judge to examine him. The dogs should be spaced so that the judge is able to move among them to see them from all angles. In practicing to "set up" or "stack" your dog for the judge's examination, bear in

Ch. Snowbank Starr Shine, son of Ch. Round Town Duke J. Ellington, is going Best of Breed at the prestigious Great Lakes Terrier event, June 1988. Handled by George Ward for Dan and Amelia Musser, Round Town Kennels, Mackinack Island, MI.

mind the importance of doing so quickly and with dexterity. The judge has a schedule to meet and only a few moments in which to evaluate each dog. You will immeasurably help yours to make a favorable impression if you are able to "get it all together" in a minimum amount of time. Practice at home before a mirror can be a great help toward bringing this about, facing the dog so that you see him from the same side that the judge will and working to make him look right in the shortest length of time.

Listen carefully as the judge describes the manner in which the dog is to be gaited, whether it is straight down and straight back; down the ring, across, and back; or in a triangle. The latter has become the most popular pattern with the majority of judges. "In a triangle" means the dog should move down the outer side of the ring to the first corner, across that end of the ring to the second corner, and then back to the judge from the second corner, using the center of the ring in a diagonal line. Please learn to do this pattern without breaking at each corner to twirl the dog around you, a senseless maneuver that has been noticed on occasion. Judges like to see the dog in an uninterrupted triangle, as they are thus able to get a better idea of the dog's gait.

It is impossible to overemphasize that the gait at which you move your dog is tremendously important and considerable study and thought should be given to the matter. At home, have someone move the dog for you at different speeds so that

you can tell which shows him off to best advantage. The most becoming action almost invariably is seen at a moderate gait, head up and topline holding. Do not gallop your dog around the ring or hurry him into a speed atypical of his breed. Nothing being rushed appears at its best; give your dog a chance to move along at his (and the breed's) natural gait. For a dog's action to be judged accurately, that dog should move with strength and power, but not excessive speed, holding a straight line as he goes to and from the judge.

As you bring the dog back to the judge, stop him a few feet away and be sure that he is standing in a becoming position. Bait him to show the judge an alert expression, using whatever tasty morsel he has been trained to expect for this purpose or, if that works better for you, use a small squeak-toy in your hand. A reminder, please, to those using liver or treats: take them with you when you leave the ring. Do not just drop them on the ground where they will be found by another dog.

When the awards have been made, accept yours graciously, no matter how you actually may feel about it. What's done is done, and arguing with a judge or stomping out of the ring is useless and a reflection on your sportsmanship. Be courteous, congratulate the winner if your dog was defeated, and try not to show your disappointment. By the same token, please be a gracious winner; this, surprisingly, sometimes seems to be still more difficult.

A little girl Westie who has really taken Westie competition by storm, this is **Ch. Glengidge Golden Charm** owned by Helene and Seymour Weiss, pictured with her handler Lanny Hirstein on the occasion of one of her frequent Terrier Group victories. Golden Charm was born June 27, 1989, a daughter of Ch. Dalriada Sam I Am ex Glengidge Golden Girl. She created considerable stir in the Montgomery Sweepstakes (the WHWTC of America Specialty) as a "starter" for her career; and since then has become a frequent Terrier Group winner in both the U.S. and Canada.

Winning a first prize in Veteran's at Montgomery County in 1980, **Ch. Sno-Bilt's Aquarius** at age ten years, bred and owned by John and Jodine Vertuno. Aquarius was sired by Dreamland's Mighty Patrol ex Ch. Sno-Bilt's Raggedee Ann.

Index

Page numbers in **boldface** refer to illustrations. For reader's convenience all championship titles and suffixes have been excluded from dogs' names.

Alastair, 91

All-Breed Dog Books From T.F.H.

H-1106, 544 pp
Over 400 color photos

H-1091, 2 Vols., 912 pp
Over 1100 color photos

TS-175, 896 pp
Over 1300 color photos

The T.F.H. all-breed dog books are the most comprehensive and colorful of all dog books available. The most famous of these recent publications, *The Atlas of Dog Breeds of the World,* written by Dr. Bonnie Wilcox and Chris Walkowicz, is now available as a two-volume set. Now in its fourth edition, the *Atlas* remains one of the most sought-after gift books and reference works in the dog world.

A very successful spinoff of the *Atlas* is the *Mini-Atlas of Dog Breeds,* written by Andrew De Prisco and James B. Johnson. This compact but comprehensive book has been praised and recommended by most national dog publications for its utility and reader-friendliness. The true field guide for dog lovers.

Canine Lexicon by the authors of the *Mini-Atlas* is an up-to-date encyclopedic dictionary for the dog person. It is the most complete single volume on the dog ever published covering more breeds than any other book as well as other relevant topics, including health, showing, training, breeding, anatomy, veterinary terms, and much more. No dog book before has ever offered this many stunning color photographs of all breeds, dog sports, and topics (over 1300 in full color!).

More Dog Books from
t.f.h. T.F.H. Publications, Inc.

H-1016, 224 pp
135 photos

H-969, 224 pp
62 color photos

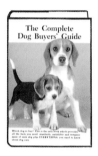

H-1061, 608 pp
Black/white photos

TS-101, 192 pp
Over 100 photos

TS-130, 160 pp
50 color illustra.

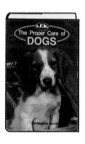

TW-102, 256 pp
Over 200 color

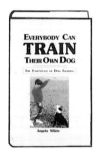

TW-113, 256 pp
200 color photos

H-962, 255 pp
Nearly 100 photos

SK-044, 64 pp
Over 50 color
photos

KW-227, 96 pp
Nearly 100 color
photos

PS-872, 240 pp
178 color illustrations

H-1095, 272 pp
Over 160 color illustrations

PS-607, 254 pp
136 Black/white photos